By Land or By Sea

By Land or By Sea

Harry J. Jacobson & Michael E. Jacobson

ISBN: 979-8-9987109-0-2 softcover
        979-8-9987109-1-9 hardcover
Library of Congress Control Number: 2025907557

Editing: Rose Shababy
Cover: Nadine L. Worden – 1955 to 2021
Illustrations: Tonia Henry (https://toniahenry.wixsite.com/design)
Layout and cover design: Kevin Miller (www.kevinmillerxi.com)

On the Edge Press® LLC
127 W 3rd St.
Port Angeles, Washington. 98362

ontheedgepress.com

Table of Contents

A WORD FROM HARRY (1926-2009)

IT IS MY sincere hope in reading through these pages that you, the reader, have a better understanding of those who choose a life at sea.

To many landlubbers, those who choose to remain on solid ground their entire life, sailors are a wild, brawling, and footloose bunch akin to a rogue wave. Not so sez I, and so shall you who take the time to read this through. Come ride the open seas and share in our adventurous spirit.

A WORD FROM MICHAEL

MY DAD WAS at sea when I was born. Being the first-born son my dad almost left his ship early to fly home. The Hosier State was berthed at a port near Bangkok Thailand. The best thing he could do was send a telegraph saying he'd be home in about thirty-five days. It was fortunate our family had a closeknit community in West Seattle in 1958, who stepped up and made sure my mom had everything she needed.

Merchant marine sailors were not paid that well at the time. When dad found another ship that paid better, he took it, even though the better pay meant he'd be gone for longer periods of time. Mom would take it all in stride as she knew what it took to be the wife of a sailor; one voyage he was gone for 6 months.

Out of the six of us, seven when our cousin came to stay with us for a while, the four older kids were expected to help with more things around the house in addition to our regular chores. When we did misbehave mom had to find a different method to make us toe the line. The most common phrase of that era was – "Just wait until your father gets home". Well, that one didn't work on us, dad may not be home for months.

When he did return mom would load the kids in the trusty station wagon and we'd go down to whatever docks the ship berthed at, usually Seattle or Ballard. Sometimes she would get there before their work was finished, meaning no one could draw their pay yet. The older boys were allowed to get out of the car and walk around the pier as long as we stayed out of trouble, and out of the way of men and equipment. One time, all seven were allowed to board the ship and sit in the galley. The cook got a real kick out of being able to get rid of the left-over meals and desserts.

The merchant marine association was founded in 1939. Governed by federal authority this fleet of privately owned vessels are controlled by the United States Maritime Administration to insure standards of international maritime laws are complied with. While not part of the military, merchant marine officers can be commissioned as military officers by the department of defense (DOD).

During peacetime this fleet primarily transports domestic and international cargo. In times of war they may be called upon to deliver military troops, material, and supplies.

In keeping with the tone of a talented poet, my dad, I felt the need to add one of my own. Here's a poem about my dad's chosen way of life and some of the things I remember from the stories he shared with all of us kids upon his return from sea.

Thirty-some-odd years,
I spent upon the sea,
Though some days it was lonely,
Always had my mates with me.

We sailed the seven seas together,
My Captain, shipmates and me,
Swapping tales and legends,
No land in sight to see.

But when my voyage is over,
And the sails will be half mast,
My soul will be of Neptune's court,
Saltwater ale will fill my glass.

By Michael Jacobson

A LIFE AT SEA

THERE ARE MANY that think the life of a sailor is a hard life in both a physical sense and to one's mental health. Of course, these thoughts usually come from people who often have no clue about what it is we really do for a living.

While our line of work as a sailor, or Able-Bodied Seaman (ABS), our official title, can be physically demanding and dangerous work at times the entire crew always had each other's backs. Our crew was often a mix of nationalities and culture; American, Russian, Lithuanian, Philippine, Haitian, just to name a few. We never seemed to have a language barrier because we respected and learned from each other. Besides, an emergency alarm is universal in any language. Each bell has a significant meaning; fire/smoke, man overboard, and abandon ship, are the main three warnings. Navigational bells, mainly used in low visibility, were understood and taught to all crewmembers as well.

Once a ship is underway, most of our working hours are spent on deck watch in twelve-hour shifts. The hardest part about a twelve-hour shift is staying alert, especially if you spent most of your off-duty hours drinking coffee and playing poker with your shipmates in the galley. I preferred to be on watch because it distracted me from thoughts of missing my family and knowing I was missed.

In the old maritime days there are five words each sailor learned as a basic code of conduct; Honesty, Discipline, Obedience, Responsibility, and Professionalism.

Honesty: Seamen are expected to be truthful and have integrity.

Discipline: Following rules and behaving in an orderly fashion is crucial.

Obedience: Respecting the chain of command and lawful orders is a key principle.

Responsibility: Caring for crew, ship property, and completing duties are important aspects.

Professionalism: This encompasses factors like punctuality, sobriety, competence, and a positive attitude towards colleagues and the maritime industry as a whole.

WHERE HAS GRANDPA GONE

Grandma, where has Grandpa gone?
Why isn't he home with me?
Don't he know I miss him?
As bad as bad can be.

Well, your Grandpa is a sailor man,
He's far out on the sea,
And I'm sure he misses you,
As bad as bad can be.

Grandpa wrote to me just yesterday,
Saying everything is quite all right,
He keeps your picture by his bed,
And kisses it each night.

Each night he hugs his pillow,
Pretending that it is you,
'Cuz to him you're very special,
He loves you through and through.

He wrote to say I love you,
Both to you and me,
To tell us that he's lonesome,
Way out there on the sea.

It's how he makes his living,
So, I guess it has to be,
But ever does he loves us,
As bad as bad can be.

DREAMS OF A SAILOR

I still remember the stories,
My Grandpa told to me,
By the quay in Boston town,
Of sailing ships and the sea.

Of merchant men and pirates,
Blackbeard's ghost, the gallows' tree,
Sending shivers up my spine,
As I sat upon his knee.

Tales of mighty clipper ships,
Barkentine, schooner and brig,
Great four-masters billowing sails,
I knew each and every rig.

In dreams I captained every one,
From rising sun to Spanish main,
Holds filled with earthly treasures,
I'd sail back home again.

Now should I go to heaven,
And the angels come for me,
I pray it's on a sailing ship,
To sail a heavenly sea.

THE SEA

My old love keeps a' calling,
Come away with me my dear,
She lures me with her beauty,
Sweet dreams of yesteryear.
My old love keeps a' calling,
Memories of distant lands,
When awake or sleeping,
She reaches for my hand.

My old love keeps a' calling,
From the beach where seagulls soar,
When the foghorns are a 'blowing,
She calls – be mine once more.

My old love keeps a' calling,
Come away again with me,
Perhaps one day I'll answer,
My old love is the sea.

A SAILOR'S LIFE

It's a lonely life, a hard life,
An old salt told to me,
It's a lonely life, a hard life,
For those that follow the sea.

Yet as oceans ever beckon,
Men 'ever heed the call,
Some return with riches,
Others never return at all.

It's a lonely life, a hard life,
Beneath the mastheads tall,
Out there beyond the land's end,
Where breakers rise and fall.

It's a lonely life, a hard life,
For loved ones left behind,
Waiting anxiously for a letter,
Saying everything is fine.

It's a lonely life, a hard life,
It's the only life I know,
Out there beyond the breakers,
Where the wild winds blow.

A SAILOR'S TATTOO

Tattoos are ever most sacred,
To those who ride the swells,
Each one a vivid reminder,
Each has a tale to tell.

Beautiful flowers or soaring birds,
On a chest a sailing ship,
Names of girls on an arm,
A tattoo to remember their lips,

Loved one's mothers and fathers,
Of the girl you left behind,
To sailors each a memory sacred,
Each tattoo is there to remind.

For a sailor's life is lonely,
Out there on a storm-tossed sea,

Now for all you tattooed rovers,
I toast fair winds to thee.

OUT TO SEA

Sticks, stones, driftwood bones,
No peddler's pack for me,
Should the devil come a' calling,
He'll find me out to sea.

Far away from the city stink,
Of garbage, rot, and swill,
Where morning gets you coughing,
From smog that's hanging still.

Out to sea you'll find me,
With things that I hold dear,
A rolling deck beneath my feet,
And sky so crystal clear.

Where a thousand stars are shining,
Upon a given night
Out to sea you'll find me,
Where everything seems right.

ONE LAST VOYAGE

Once again on a rolling deck,
Oh, how I long to be,
Stout companions at my side,
Wild winds blowing free.

Kinship with the world again,
Friend of porpoise and whale,
Upon the vast expanse,
I would bid this land farewell.

Setting sails for distant shores,
Old acquaintance to renew,
Mabe Singapore or Hong Kong,
Where we'll lift a cup or two.

Perhaps in old Calcutta,
I'll find a familiar face,
Thailand's blessed with dancing girls,
Moving beauty and grace.

In Japan I'll have some saki,
Served with Geisha's smile,
There in cherry blossom land,
I think I shall linger awhile.

Then off to Australia's shore,
Where girls are dinkum best,
From there on to the Philippines,
With old friends I'll reminisce.

In Tahiti and Hawaii,
I'll have myself a time,
Then I'll go through Panama,
Got Europe on my mind.

Now when my journey's over,
The anchor's planted on my lawn,
I'll probably wish for one last voyage,
And then to settle down.

A LOVE AND HATE AFFAIR

There's many a name I called ye',
Wild bitch or bloody whore,
A crazy love and hate affair,
Ye damn well gets me sore.

Ya chews me up an' spits me out,
I keeps coming back for more,
And ye been a doing it,
A going past four score.

One day I'm going to leave ya,
I swears by my tattoo,
Let some other bloody bugger,
Sing his songs to you.
And I'll be off to Fiddler's green,
Packing on my shoulder an oar,
I'll know damn well I've arrived,
When folks ask what it's for.

Then we'll see who missed who,
Ya wild and bloody whore,
When ye calls me, I won't be there,
I won't be there no more.

Dammit somehow I won't be there,
It just don't seem quite right,
We been lovers much too long,
An' what's a lover's fight.

So please accept my apology,
My beautiful and lovely sea,
When you calls - I promise,
I'll come back to thee.

That's the way of a sailor's life,
A love and hate affair,
Somehow the oceans always wins,
I know 'cause I been there.

DRIFTWOOD

Gnarled, battered, by sea and surf,
Driftwood bobbing off the beach,
Hope and chance of survival,
Somehow, forever — just of reach.

For now, the tide is changing,
Carrying you out to sea again,
Will there ever be another time,
And what will happen then?

Will it be as it was before,
Driftwood bobbing close to shore,
Drifting, bobbing, close to shore,
Until the time of evermore?

Or perhaps will someone see,
The innate beauty that's in ye,
Lifts you up with loving hands,
And forever cherishes thee.

Ah, so much like you, my friend,
Like driftwood on the sea,
Ever close, but yet so far,
For someone wanting me.

THANKSGIVING AT SEA

Happy Thanksgiving sez I too he,
Happy for what sez he to me,
Happiness is home with family,
Not here on the bloody sea.

Well, sez I, Thanksgiving to me,
Is only what ya make it to be,
Whether home upon the land,
Or out on the bloody sea.

Now if ya' thinks it over,
I'm sure you will agree,
There's many a darn good reason,
For Thanksgiving on the sea.

Aye, it's true sez he to me,
Happy Thanksgiving to ye,
So, responding once again,
Happy Thanksgiving sez I to he.

A SAILOR TO HIS LOVE

I know it's hard to understand,
Why I can't be home with you,
But it's also hard for me,
Because I love you too.

I carry your picture in my heart,
With me wherever I go,
I miss you always darling,
Somehow, I'm sure you know.
You'll always be my sweetheart,
You will always have my love,
I ever pray for angels,
To guide you from above.

And when my journey's over,
I'll give a hug and kiss,
To one that I've been lonesome for,
Lonesome for and missed.

THE SEAMAN'S CODE

I learned it many years ago,
When I first went to sea,
After signing of the articles,
A code was given to me.

A code for men to live by,
When the sea is their abode,
Amongst the ocean's brotherhood,
It's known as the seaman's code.

The seaman's code is one of love,
And respect for one another,
Know ye upon the sea,
Each of us are brothers.

Five simple words, yet binding,
They're good enough for me,
For all mankind are brothers,
No matter where they be.

A SPECIAL BREED

There's a very special breed of men,
Who for the ocean's bounty search,
Scanning horizons from weathered decks,
Like eagles from a lofty perch.

A special breed, the fishermen,
Who brave the windswept sea,
Undaunted by tempestuous weather,
A tribute to all men free.

Spirit of America kept alive,
These stout God-fearing men,
Knowing full well each season,
Some will never return again.

Yet ever do they venture out,
Time after time again,
In search of the ocean's treasure,
This special breed of men.

TALKING TO YOUR PICTURE

I'm talking to your picture,
Telling you how much I care,
How I long to hold you,
And wish that I were there.

Outside a gale is blowing wild,
In here with you I'm warm,
Though our ship is being battered,
By the fierceness of the storm.

Snug and warm with you my dear,
And not the least afraid.
Got your picture on my pillow,
Where my head is laid.
I'm talking to your picture,
Of another time and place,
When we pledged a love forever,
And in our love embraced.

I still can feel your body,
Arms and legs entwined,
Two hearts beating close together,
In rapture, yours and mine.

SOUTH SEA DREAMS

Down in the South Sea islands,
Where the weather's mostly fair,
With beautiful girls, swaying palms,
I'd like to settle there.

There to while away my days,
Like a bloody old salt should,
Maybe get me a little harem,
Plant me anchor for good.

And should ya' come a calling,
I'll welcome you for fair,
To come aboard, rest a bit,
Forget about your cares.

Got a bottle on the shelf,
Of good ole mountain dew,
And one sweet little wahine,
Awaiting just for you.

SHIPMATES AND SPECIAL PEOPLE

IN EVERYONE'S LIFE, there are certain people who are unforgettable, shining out in one's memory like a star. In my life at sea there have been many, though most are gone now. Through hurricanes, storms, and tempest, we sailed together. Shipmates on the voyage to eternity, where perhaps we shall meet again someday to reminisce about the brotherhood of the sea.

The last poem in this chapter is about a wonderful lady who sailed off many years ago with her husband, in search of a dream. Together, they made it come true.

On a barren beach, just outside of Honolulu, they built a paradise. When her husband died people tried to take it away from her and forced her to move. When she did, she took every flower, plant, tree, and blade of grass with her keeping their dream alive. Knowing her has given me the strength to continue in the fulfillment of my own.

TO A SHIPMATE

Shipmates once are forever,
In a brotherhood that binds,
By wind and majestic oceans,
Bonded together for all time.
So never farewell but later,
'til we sail together again,
Once again in the brotherhood,
Of stout seafaring men.

'Til we sail together again,
Upon a windswept sea,
With porpoise riding on the bow,
A toast from you to me.

A toast to pleasant memories,
From both the ship and crew,
As sailormen never say goodbye,
Until later friend, adieu.

HERB PADILLA

Aye' you can tell by his manner,
A man for all seasons is he,
A right and proper bos'n,
Who knows of ships and sea.

I speak of Herb Padilla,
A real man's man he be,
Respected by the whole darn crew,
Including old salts like me.

Aye' he be of the brotherhood,
A breed of men apart,
Who make their living on the sea,
And seamanship an art.

Soon our journey will be over,
We'll go our separate ways,
But I'd consider it an honor,
To meet another day.

TOMMY DEES

Tommy Dees or salty dog,
It makes no never mind,
Whatever names you call him,
He's really one of a kind.

The ocean is his lady fair,
And that she'll always be,
The stars and sky his treasures,
His castle a ship on the sea.

Now Tommy's tried to settle down,
Maybe a time or three,
'Til he hears a whistle blow,
Come away old friend with me.

Then it's adios my loved one,
I hope you will understand,
Love you, but I got to go,
For I'm a seafaring man.

Wives and kids are lonely,
What the hell, so are we,
That's why today I give a salute,
To the sailor Tommy Dees.

BOS'N BILL

Some folks call him Bos'n Bill,
I calls em from the heart,
An' that's the way it oughta be,
A giving all, not part.

From the heart's his motto,
It is his code of the sea,
A darn good code to live by,
From the heart, respectfully.

All for one, one for all,
Be damned to tempest or storm,
From the heart on deck together,
A brotherhood was formed.

A brotherhood of seamen,
Bos'n Bill a toast to thee,
From the heart of a shipmate,
Is how it's gotta be.

SOUNDS LIKE CALLAHAN

You say Callahan is the Captain,
I say it cannot be,
Tell me Laddy, tell me,
Describe the man to me.

Is his 'air black as coal,
The front of his 'ead most bare,
Sure, it sounds like Callahan,
'Yer description fits 'em fair.
'As he a twinkle e'en his eye,
A grin from 'air to 'air,
Sure, it sounds like Callahan,
The one I knew back there.

Does he sometimes wear a kilt,
Ladies say a Kaber's thar,
Sure, it sounds like Callahan,
But I 'eard he crossed the bar.

The Callahan I 'usta knew,
Was scalawag and rover too,
His dance it was the hornpipe,
And his ballads mor'en a few.

Yet I 'eard they hung 'em,
Somewhere south of Inisfree,
But it sure sounds like Callahan,
What 'yer describing to me.

Buy me another drink Laddy,
Barmaid fill the blooming glass,
For it sure sounds like Callahan,
Or a ghost from otta his past.

TO A SPECIAL PERSON

I knew you were someone special,
From the moment that we met,
You had that very special look,
It was a pleasure meeting Annette.
Down to earth real people,
I appreciated your humor and wit,
Then looking a little closer,
I found you had true grit.
To have a very special dream,
And then make it come true,
Takes a lot of doing,
True grit through and through.

Most dreams are only falling stars,
A wish on starlit nights,
That's why to me you're special,
You kept your dream in sight.

It was a pleasure and an honor,
An honor to have met,
A very special person,
My best to you, Annette.

ON CROSSING THE EQUATOR

THE FOLLOWING TWO poems were written for initiation ceremonies. Upon crossing the equator it is customary to initiate novice seamen, or wogs, as they are sometimes called, bringing them before Neptune's court for trial. Those found worthy will become shellbacks, following a tradition carried on from the days of sailing ships.

Being a shellback and scribe of Neptune's court I am sworn to keep secret all details of what takes place during these ceremonies. Perhaps someday, if you dare venture forth across the vast Pacific, you will find out for yourself.

WARNING TO A WOG

Davey Jones lies in waiting,
More devil than a man,
Waiting for good ships and men,
Bringing death to all he can.

Death to all foolish intruders,
Who dare to brave the sea,
Unwary snatched from rolling decks,
In his graveyard now they be.

Now they be forevermore,
Bound tight by Davey's chains,
Along with some of the finest ships,
That ever sailed the main.

Take heed you wogs and wiggly's,
To an ancient mariner this day,
Lest a loved one sits a weeping,
Upon some lonely Quay.

Only one thing Davey's 'fraid of,
And that tis Neptune's wrath,
So, seek shelter in his brotherhood,
If on the sea you'd last.

Be initiated into his kingdom,
A kingdom mighty and vast,
Ol' Davey's swear an' cus ya,
While wogs, now seamen, laugh.

A LETTER TO NEPTUNE'S COURT

We brings before ye on this day,
Aye, a sight that's worse than sore,
Our good ships filled wi' scumbag wogs,
We's got 'em by the score.

Not e'en fit for gallows tree,
Lower 'en a slug's slick slimy trail,
I swear, not e'en ol' Davey,
Will take 'em o'er his rail.

But they's here and here we brung 'em,
To be judged by you this day,
Like your orders say to do,
With all wogs who come your way.

Personally, I sez, do 'em in,
Cat 'o nine tails or the yard,
Let the scavengers pick their bones,
'Til nothings left but a shard.

A lesson to all scumbag wogs,
To those who would your kingdom trespass,
If they aint got what a sailor's made of,
Let it be their bloody arse.

MYSTERIOUS TALES

THE SEA HAS been a source of mystery since the first man set sail. To this very day tales of strange and mysterious creatures, from mermaids to sea monsters, are still recalled wherever men gather together on the waterfronts of the world.

I myself can bear witness to many strange and fearful happenings and have many a shipmate to be afeard of venturing forth upon the deck after night falls, especially when crossing the Bermuda Triangle. And it's no wonder with the tales that prevail, stories of ships found floatin' with no trace of the entire crew. No trace of crew and of entire ships disappearing. And, for no apparent reason, the appearance of ghost ships with ghostly apparitions standin' at the rail. Aye, the sea has its stories, I say for one, too many to be discounted.

MARE TENEBROSOM

Mare Tenebrosom, incarnate with Satan,
A dreadful sea of lost souls,
Where ships and sailors disappear,
And stories of horror unfold.

Some say it's the Bermuda Triangle,
Literally the sea of darkness I'm told,
Whatever, I'm here to warn you,
Of the evil and terror it holds.

For I am the lone survivor,
Of the schooner Nancy Deare,
All the rest are dead and gone,
Their screams still ring in my ears.

We were in the Bermuda Triangle,
Becalmed in a fog bound sea,
When all of a sudden it happened,
It still burns in my memory.

Over the gunnels came apparitions,
Apparitions of demons from hell,
With wicked knives they hacked and cut,
'Til none were left to tell.

None left to tell what happened,
None left to tell but me,
Apparently, they thought me dead,
When I fell into the sea.

I beg of you heed my warning,
Of dark in the Devil's sea,
Lest you be not so fortunate,
So fortunate as me.

VENGENCE AT SEA

Halloween aboard the Thomas Sim Lee,
Tramp steamer rusty and old,
Long past due for the boneyard,
A story of death was told.

A story of vengeance and rendered,
On the eve of all souls' day,
Where even on the ocean deep,
Spirits of dead hold sway.

A seaman cursed for falsehood,
An oath of vengeance swore,
By an innocent man condemned,
To die on a foreign shore.

I swear I'll come to get you Jack,
From the depths where ashes lie,
Upon a hallowed eve I'll come,
Come to watch you die.

Words to haunt a memory,
I'll come to watch you die,
Many a night from shadows Jack,
Felt watched by ghostly eyes.

'Til that Hallowed eve on lookout,
Jack's fears were justified,
Out of the fog an apparition came,
With cold bone chilling eyes.

Aye, it was as curse foretold,
The one he condemned with a lie,
Standing there with finger pointing,
To watch Jack — in horror die.

When Jack's face, a death mask frozen,
The ghostly figure turned away,
And into the darkness softly spoke,
Father, you've been avenged today.

Jack's diary told the story,
Of betrayal and the curse,
And how fear of retribution,
Caused his heart to burst.

A GHOSTLY TALE

There's many strange and eerie tale,
Comes from the Spanish main,
Of ghostly ships and pirates,
Told over and over again.

Of nether spirits who cannot sleep,
'Til evil has been atoned,
A curse upon their bloody heads,
Cursed forevermore to roam.

To roam the seas they plundered,
Lest they somehow make amends,
By seeing that their treasures found,
And used for a goodly end.
Blackbeard's ghost many times appeared,
Only to frighten his savior away,
And the ghost of Kingston market,
Still appears both night and day.

They say it's the ghost of Morgan,
That his treasures buried there,
A looking for a goodly man,
To lift the curse he bears.

I wonder on a spindrift night,
Should a pirate's ghost appear,
And I had the courage,
Would I, of his treasures hear.

Perhaps it's just a story,
Then again perhaps 'tis true,
Whatever should you believe or not,
It's really up to you.

THE FLYING DUTCHMAN

When a rounding the Cape of Good Hope,
Upon a storm-tossed night,
A ghostly ship came sailing by,
Sailing in the pale moonlight.

She were a three masted schooner,
Her sails were a bloody red,
Neath her bowsprit you could see,
A most ghastly figurehead.

Me and my shipmates we crossed ourselves,
Her name you could plainly see,
It was the Fliegend Hollander,
The Flying Dutchman ship she be.

She came about and crowded us,
Close on our starboard side,
Deliver these the Dutchman said,
Tossing a packet in oilskin tied.

Deliver these and save yer 'selves,
From the shoals that lie ahead,
Refuse me and I promise,
That ye all will soon be dead.

Deliver these and lift the curse,
That binds me to the sea,
These letters asking forgiveness,
Deliver them, that I'll be free.

MOTHER CAREY

Many strange tales at sea are told,
But what I say to you is truth,
A truth from days of old,
Truth to make yer blood run cold.
Of the sea witch Mother Carey,
A monster who roams the sea,
She'll eat yer eyes an' drink yer blood,
If you should unwary be

Some say a witch or vampire,
Others, the worst of Banshee,
Whatever lads, it be the truth,
And that you can take from me.

I seen her just once I tell ya,
Just once and that aint no lie,
In the shadows where the lookout stands,
She were eating me shipmate's eyes.

If it weren't for my sailor's cross,
I too would have been her fare,
But onc't her eyes fell upon it,
She disappeared into the air.

Now should you on a spindrift night,
Be strolling on the deck,
Beware of what lurks in the shadows,
Lest Carey's fingers find yer neck.

OF LEGENDS

As THE MYSTERIES of the sea prevail, so do its legends. I would be hard pressed to write of them all in my lifetime.

Like its mysteries, the legends of the sea can neither be confirmed or discounted. I leave these things for you, the reader, to decide for yourself. Of the many superstitions, I swears by my tattoo they are all valid, same as I do for ghosts and other strange happenings.

LEGEND OF THE GOLDEN EARING

From Scottish lore in days of old,
There's a story that is told,
Of an ancient Scottish fisherman,
And an earring made of gold.

Each day out from Saint Andrews bay,
The fishermen in his dory rowed,
Each day death's icy fingers,
Reached for the Scotsman ever cold.

Each day to church his good wife,
Went to kneel in fervent prayer,
Asking God and angels,
Her husband's life to spare.

'Til one day in answer,
In answer to her prayers,
An angel came unto her,
To comfort and to care.

In her hand a golden earring,
To protect her husband dear,
Let him wear it in his ear,
Hence more you need not fear.

So 'tis down through ancient history
There's many a sailor you'll see,
A wearing a golden earring,
Blessed by the heavens that be.

A LEGEND FROM WHERE OCEANS MEET

It was down near Nono-Uti,
Where the story first was told,
Of a beautiful island princess,
And her love in days of old.

She loved the chief Kuria,
He her love returned tenfold,
They were pledged to be united,
Where the oceans meet and hold.

Little did the lovers know,
Death flags would soon unfurl,
For scalawags were in search of,
Nono-Uti's fabled pearls.

Black pearls from the murky depths,
Of a shark infested reef,
Where diving was declared taboo,
For treasure gained through grief.
The captured the chief of Kuria,
Held in ransom his princess fair,
Lest he dive for black pearls,
Her life they would not spare.

So, into death's murky waters,
He went time and time again,
His love for her much greater,
Than the fear he held within.

Sharks were gathering for the kill,
When the princess broke and dove,
Choosing death with him she loved,
Hand and hand they swam below.

The sea gods moved with passion,
So, the story is told,
Made them rulers of the sea,
Where the oceans meet and hold.

Now all who cross the water,
Between Nono-Uti and Kuria,
Must make offering for safe passage,
Or ever rue the day.

THE LEGEND OF DAVEY JONES

Legends don't just happen,
Circumstances make 'em grow,
Through the devil and Davey's dad,
A tale that you should know.

Davey Jones and his locker,
A true story of the sea,
It aint no lie I tell ya,
Here's how it came to be.

Fate has a way of playing tricks,
As we all know it can,
So it were with Davey Jones,
When the devil dealt a hand.

His daddy was a gambler,
And a helleva fighter too,
Won his wife with a deck of cards,
I swears by my tattoo.

Still, they loved each other,
Even though it took some time,
But trouble was a coming,
Like a fast freight down the line.

Now bad luck runs in bunches,
It's fact as we all know,
A pregnant wife, a broken arm,
And cash a running low.

So, with one thing or the other,
Pickins were getting mighty slim,
That's when the devil came along,
With a proposition for him

Well, not so right away it was,
It were gonna take some time,
But the devil is a slick one,

So, he really did not mind.

I hear you are a gambler,
The devil to his daddy sez,
And when it comes to gambling,
Folks say, yer the best that is.

Davey's dad, he were flattered,
As flattered as can be,
In my time I beat the best,
But how'd you know 'bout me?

The devil hadn't given his name,
Hadn't give his name 'til then,
The gambler said, I had a hunch,
That you just might be him.

I said that I could beat you,
And I still think I can,
So, if you came to gamble,
Get the cards and deal a hand.

Night and day they gambled,
Finally, the gambler bet it all,
The devil gave a little grin,
And said I got to call.

The gambler had three aces,
The devil's were all red,
Drawing three cards to a flush,
Just aint done, the gambler said.

I don't know how you did it,
I got nothing else to lose,
But I gotta give you credit,
Ya damn well earned your dues.

The devil said, yer in a fix,
Your wife being pregnant and all,

But if you accept my proposition,
I'll build you a gambling hall.
A gambling hall and fancy saloon,
Right here on this very dock,
Where all the sailors come ashore,
To spend what e're they got.

All I ask is that you pledge,
Pledge your soul to me,
Then all that I have promised,
I will give to ye.

The gambler thought it over,
Said, I'll give my soul to you,
Unless my child beats the devil,
By the time he's twenty-two.

The devil thought, I beat the father,
I can surely beat the son,
With a grin upon his face,
He said the deal is done.

Twenty-two years the gambler spoke,
Plenty of time to find a way,
You'll never do it the devil replied,
I'll see you in hell that day.

Davey's mother died soon after,
A short time after his birth,
She got atween two sailors fighting,
The devil had done his worst.

The gambler's life was turning sour,
In spite of his newfound wealth,
Without your love beside you,
All gold is merely pelf.

He wished he hadn't gambled,
With the devil on that day,

61

A wise man once had told him,
When you play you gotta play.
What will I do with Davey,
How'm I gonna raise my son,
Gambling is one tough business,
A boy sure needs his mom.

He'd been walking and a worrying,
Back and forth along the quay,
There must be something I can do,
I just gotta find a way.

I can help you find it,
A voice spoke, soft, yet clear,
I've been sent to help you,
Solve your problems here.

I've been sent by Father Neptune,
My Father and my King,
At the bidding of your God,
To help undo the devil's thing.

He cheated you, and had a hand,
In taking your Mary away,
And should you not be wary,
Your son, Davey, he will slay.

For Davey is your salvation,
The devil knows it well,
Unless we can protect him,
You'll find yourself in Hell.

Up from the water rose a mermaid,
As lovely as a picture can be,
Don't be alarmed she told him,
Please don't be afraid of me.

Put your son into my care,
To keep him safe from harm,

He can live beneath the ocean,
I have cast a magic charm.
Let the devil think Davey's drowned,
So he'll no longer bother you,
When it's safe for his return,
We'll give the devil his cue.

That's how Davey became a member,
Of King Neptune's royal clan,
He could breathe beneath the ocean,
As well as on the land.
King Neptune's daughter taught him,
Taught him how to read and write,
Then her father took a hand,
And taught him how to fight.
How to fight and gamble,
'Til he were the very best,
For Neptune knew the devil,
Would put him to the test.

Soon Davey were a wrestlin' sharks,
Sharks and sea monsters too,
He wrestled and he tamed 'em,
Like no other one could do.

It were on his sixteenth birthday,
Neptune called to bid him good-bye,
Saying, yer as ready as can be,
To give the devil a try.

So back to the world of sunshine,
Of sunshine and blue skies,
Where his father were awaiting,
There was tears in both their eyes.
It's time to call the devil,
Time to give 'em the news,
That I'm alive and ready,
Ready to give him what's due.

Well, Davey beat the devil,
He did it up right fine,
Dealt himself a royal flush,
Gave the devil a pair of nines.

One time the devil played him,
For all those lost at sea,
And dear friend's the story,
Of how Davey's locker came to be.

So it is with due respect,
Down where Neptune's kingdom lays,
We stop a while and pay a tribute,
Before going on our way.

A SAILOR'S TALE

One day, a strolling dockside,
I espied a seafaring man,
Denim jeans and stripped shirt,
Tattoos on both his hands.

Beneath his neckerchief 'bout his head,
From his ear, a golden earring band,
Curiosity got the better of me,
As ya know it damn well can.

So, I hailed 'em up an' asked 'em,
Please tell me my good man,
Why do sailors in their ears,
Wear them golden bands.

He sez to me, my Laddy,
See that thar yonder Inn,
Arter ye buys a dram or two,
Maybe be I can fill ye in.

'Twas there he told the story,
'Tis gospel and 'tis true,
This here's what he told me,
I swears by my tattoo.

It was given by the angels,
That all good sailors should wear,
A ring from earlobe hanging,
To ward off death out there.

He were lookin' outa the window,
Wi' a cold and ghostly stare,
And after we had another,
He jest up and disappeared.

THE DEVIL AND DAVEY JONES

Davey Jones was once a seaman,
As most any, with knowledge knows,
But how he got his Kingdom,
Has hardly ever been told.

So, I'm going to tell ye,
Jest like Davey told to me,
Sez I were a shipwrecked,
On the Southernmost of seas.

There weren't no other survivors,
I were the onliest that be,
Sitting there upon me raft,
Singing a song of Fiddle Dee Dee.

When the devil comes a swimmin',
Swimmin' by in search of souls,
He up's and sits beside me,
Wi' tha' look a one who knows.

Quick he spies me deck o' cards
I had laying out to dry,
He sez, how about a little game,
To make the time go by.

An' that's how Davey got his Kingdom,
Down there beneath the sea,
When a gamblin' with the devil,
He had aces up his sleeve.

A LEGENDARY SAILOR

They calls me the ancient mariner,
Sometimes I think it's so,
Been sailing nigh forever,
And still I'm on the go.

'Round the horn and back again,
I've sailed from pole to pole,
Up and down and all around,
Been from Maine to Mexico.

Like Pecos Bill and Bunyan,
I too a legend be,
'Ceptin they were on the land,
While I be of the sea.

I once lassoed a hurricane,
Just for a little tow,
When the durn thing turned about,
I had to let her go.

Now, I hates to be a braggin',
But facts is facts you see,
Them other legends I mentioned,
Aint half as brave as me.

Why, all them beautiful islands,
Ya' find in the Southern seas,
Were all kicked up from down below,
By my old sea horse and me.

At's when I were a taming him,
He 'et some loco seaweed,
An' most typhoons get their start,
From ridin' that ol' steed.

So, you see, as legends go,
And facts are as they be,
Me an' my sea horse Percy,

Are legends of the sea.

There's many a tale me Laddy's
I may tell another day,
But I hears a mermaid calling,
And must be on my way.

So, until another day,
I swears by my tattoo,
There's many more sea stories,
An' all of them are true.

WHISTLING 'N CUPS

Ye can call it superstition,
But for fact I know 'tis true,
There's two things on the ocean,
A good seaman just don't do.

One's a whistling on a bridge,
Other's one cup facing another,
Each can cause a terrible tempest,
I kid you nor dear brother.

Fearsome hurricanes and waterspouts,
Enough to turn you inside out,
Caused by a careless sailorman,
Who turned his cup about.

And there's many that'll tell ye',
'Bout whistling up a storm,
Terrible disasters out at sea,
Loved ones with hearts a torn.

So be careful all ye' sailormen,
Be careful in your ways,
'Lest in Davey Jone's locker,
Ye' find yerself someday.

Never whistle on a bridge,
Or turn yer cup around,
Fair skies 'll be yer blessing,
Fer taking advice most sound.

A SPIRIT WILD AND FREE

I am here, there, everywhere,
Yet my face you cannot see,
Whatever my whim or fancy,
I can do with thee.

I can tear a house apart,
Sink a ship upon the sea,
When I'm in a different mood,
I can so gentle be.

So gentle and so loving,
Each touch a gentle caress,
I can bring a flower's fragrance,
Each on at my behest.

Yet man can never tame me,
Like a will 'o the wisp I be,
For I am the spirit of the wind,
Ever wild and free.

THE WIDOWMAKER WIND

Most sailormen are wise,
In knowledge of wind and sea,
Ever watchful, ever cautious,
Should they have longevity.

For those are unwary,
Davey Jone's locker awaits,
Only the finest for the sea,
Lesser men rue their fate.

Each ocean has its graveyards,
Each had fearful winds,
But in the reaches of Alaska,
There's one the devil's kin.

The devil's kin awaiting,
To do the careless in,
Seemingly from hell itself,
'Tis the windowmakers' wind.

Oldtimers know and fear it,
The young and restless laugh,
'Till the widowmaker reaches out,
Deadly fingers for their craft.

When the riffled sea turns calm,
And seagulls disappear,
When distant peaks are magnified,
The widowmaker wind is near.

So, listen well you reckless ones,
Heed what old-timers say,
Lest your widow sit a crying,
Upon some lonely quay.

JUST FOR FUN

AYE, JUST FOR fun I titled these, yet there's truth on every page. Many a time in Magen's Bay on the beach I lay, just a talking to a pirate's ghost or a sweet comely maid. And it's true, I have the treasure map of the scoundrel Billy Bones, and for a price I'll share it with you alone. As for Pooka's and for mermaids, I've only known a few. An' ya darn well can believe me, I swears by my tattoo.

BILL'S LAST TALE

Ol' Bill he was my partner,
I know he would'na lie,
This here's what he told me,
Lookin' straight into my eye.

He said, Jake I gotta tell ye,
Can't hold it in no more,
Gotta tell ya just what happened,
When strollin' by the shore.

I heard a voice a callin',
A callin' me I swear,
Looking up I saw a mermaid,
Sittin' in the water there.

A sittin' on a rock awash,
There in the moonlit sea,
Her arms and voice a beckoning,
Come closer Bill to me.

Jake, it were my true love,
Who died so long ago,
She pledged upon her deathbed,
That she'd never let me go.

Well Jake, I gotta be with her,
I can't be apart no more,
Perhaps someday we'll meet again,
Upon some distant shore.

A TALE OF A SAILOR
(sung to the tune of Midnight on the Ocean)

Come sit beside me Laddy,
And I'll tell you a tale of the sea,
Of mysterious and magical creatures,
People say just cannot be.

Of Mother Carey the sea witch,
I've seen her once or twice,
Davey Jones and me were shipmates,
I taught him how to splice.

Once I almost married a mermaid,
The courtship was touch and go,
She couldn't live upon the land,
I couldn't live below.

Long John Silver was me friend,
I knew the pirate Captain Kidd,
For a price I'll draw a map,
Showing where their treasures hid.

Oh, hear the tale of a sailor,
Hear a tale of the sea,
I'll tell you of sea monsters,
And the whale who swallowed me.

Now all you sweet young ladies,
If great lovers you would be,
I'll be glad to teach you,
What a mermaid taught to me.

Oh, hear the tale of a sailor,
Hear a tale of the sea,
I'll be glad to teach you,
I'll even do it for free.

Oh, hear the tale of a sailor,
Hear a tale of the sea,

Oh, hear the tale of a sailor,
I'll tell you what happened to me.

One night a skinny dipping,
Down there off the beach,
I felt something a tickling,
A tickling my feet.

I looked down in the water,
A mermaid I did see,
She were just a laying there,
A smiling up at me.

Oh, hear the tale of a sailor,
Hear a tale of the sea,
Oh, hear the tale of a sailor,
I'll tell you what happened to me.
Oh, hear the tale of a sailor,
Hear a tale of the sea,
Pardon me for saying,
It's a bunch of boloney.

Now sailors are good for good times,
Good times and fun they be,
But when the party's over,
Toss 'em back in the sea.

Once I loved a sailor,
He said I were the only one,
He had a girl in every port,
The dirty son of a gun.

Oh, hear the tale of a sailor,
Hear a tale of the sea,
But never trust the buggers,
Take it straight from me.

AN ORDINARY TALE

A working on a survey ship,
With a scientific sorta crew,
A Captain that were Irish,
And all the sailors crazy too.

All 'cept me my darling,
I swears by my tattoo,
And of course, me pooka,
Who's most as big as you.

We sailed North from Seattle,
To Alaska's frozen shore,
That's where I met the pooka,
Frozen stiff as a board.

I took 'em aboard an' thawed 'em,
As any Samaritan would do,
When he 'eard we're headed South,
He said I'm coming wi you.

Now no one else can see him,
Nary a one but me,
Pooka's never appear to anyone,
Unless good friends they be.

Me shipmates think me crazy,
As crazy as can be,
Just because they heard us singing,
A bats in the old belfry.

One day the pooka promised,
He'd appear to the whole damn crew,
When he does, we'll be the same,
Ordinary through and through.

A TALE OF THE SPANISH MAIN

Gather 'round me lads and lassies,
I'll tell you a tale of the sea,
Of meeting the ghost of Billy Bones,
And the map he gave to me.

Once when sailing the Spanish Main,
In search of wealth and treasure,
I dropped me hook in Magen's Bay,
To rest a bit and pleasure.

Like old time pirates usta do,
Morgan, Drake, Blackbeard and more,
A dropping their hooks same as I,
Then off to Saint Thomas ashore.

Blackbeard had a castle there,
With a tower overlooking the sea,
And a spyglass pointing outward,
A bloody place of infamy

Aye, a place of infamy,
In those wild pirate days,
Today it be a paradise,
In much more peaceful ways.

One evening full and rested,
Sitting alone, out on the quay,
I were approached by a stranger,
I'll remember all my days.

He were dirty, old, and ragged,
Smelled a tha' salty sea,
Atween a dance and a shuffle,
He sidled up to me.

His face were weather beaten,
A patch o'er one a his eyes
T'other glowed like fire from hell,

He seemed one who would'na die.

I must confess being shaken,
Out there on the quay alone,
Especially when he said he were,
The ghost of Billy Bones.

He said I been here for ages,
A watching out to sea,
Waitin' for one that was promised,
Promised to set me free.

On a sloop shipshape in Bristol,
He'd drop his hook in tha' bay,
An' one evening I wud find 'em,
A sitting alone on tha' quay.

Wi that he hands me a parchment,
A treasure map sez he,
Spend it wisely and fer good,
My blessings go wi thee.

Now I'm still a searching,
While Billy Bones is free,
'Cause I can't find the island,
Where the treasures 'sposed to be.

ANSWERING AN ADVERTISMENT

A thumbing through a magazine,
I came across these ads,
Saying poems and songs are wanted,
We needs 'em all, real bad.

Send 'em to a box it said,
It did not make much sense,
I got a whole durn box full,
And still aint got one cent.

After reading through a page,
I found there were only two,
Who even had an address,
That's why I sent 'em to you.
'Cause if them other fellows,
Only got a box like me,
I sure hope they's careful,
Not to fall otta the tree.

I aint really sent 'em yet,
Because I'm out upon the sea,
But as soon as I make a homeport,
I'll send a packet to ye,

And if I don't get an answer,
I'll think about the trees,
Just perhaps they might be,
A whole lot saner than me

But please if you must use paper,
Don't make 'em out of trees.

TO A LOVED ONE

LOVE POEMS HAVE always sacred from the beginning of time. Especially for seafarers and other roving kinds should they want a lovely miss to keep them on her mind. So, we write and tell them of our undying love and swear, they are the only one beneath the stars above. For life is hard and lonely out on a storm-tossed sea and all the time yer dreaming about someone loving ye.

TO MY LOVE

When the seas are stormy,
And night winds are blowing cold,
I pretend that you're beside me,
Where I can touch and hold.

There I tell you of my love,
Of the hurt within my heart,
Oh God, how much I miss you,
How hard it was to part.

I couldn't tell you then dear,
I just smiled and said goodbye,
I'm lonesome and I love you,
I need you by my side.

When I see you once again,
I'll hold you ever so tight,
And tell darling of my love,
Each and every night.

A LOVE POEM

I would that I could give you,
The world within in your arms,
If I but had the power,
I would cast a magic charm.

Then silk, satin, fancy dress,
Exotic furs and such,
Motor cars and mansions,
Would never be too much.

Yet, I know it cannot be,
It is all beyond my means,
For you I'll have to find a gift,
From my treasure trove of dreams.

From deep within a secret place,
Where special things are stored,
Lies a package with your name,
Tied with a silver cord.

A card that says I love you,
Is attached to tell I care,
Within the package is a heart,
I'll always with you share.

I MISS YOU

I miss you dear, I love you,
Is all that I can say,
'Til I hold you in my arms,
On a very special day.

Special because I'll have you,
Here close within my arms,
To tell you darling of my love,
And keep you safe from harm.

It's hard to be away my dear,
So lonely when we're apart,
Whenever I think about you,
There's an ache within my heart.

So 'til I hold you once again,
On that very special day,
I love you and I miss you,
Is all that I can say.

FOR YOU

Yesterday I went searching,
To find a gift for you,
In the very best of stores,
Yet nothing there would do.

I wanted something special,
That money could not buy,
To put a smile on your face,
A twinkle in your eye.

So away to memories lane,
Unto my treasure hoard,
Again, I went a searching,
Where the best is stored.

I selected from the finest,
Love, care, and happiness too,
Carefully wrapped in my heart,
All the best for you.

NIGHT AND DAY

Each night I say I love you,
Before I go to bed,
Then I say it once again,
Before I nod my head.

In dreams I ever hold you,
There deep within my heart,
I love you makes things better,
With each new day I start.

Whether on the ocean deep,
Or a distant Port of Call,
Night and day from my heart,
Three words say it all.

FROM THE SHORE

EVEN BETWEEN VOYAGES a true seafarer is never far from his love. You'll find him strolling on the waterfront or on a perch overlooking the harbor, ofttimes beachcombing, sometimes sailing or rowing a dory. Whatever or wherever, he'll never be far away. At sea he dreams of land, on shore he longs for the sea. Even though I be a seafarer it's still perplexing to me.

SUNRISE OVER SEATTLE

When the sun rises over Seattle,
A breathtakingly splendid view,
I sit in rapture across the bay,
Captured by its beauty anew.

How many times, I cannot you,
I've watched the panorama unfold,
From my perch o'er Duwamish head Bay,
A sight that never grows old.

First the Space Needle begins to shine,
To bask in the morning's first light,
Then it calls to the city,
To rise up out of the night.

Now I see a ferry at the dock,
Ready to make its first run,
Across the Sound to Bremerton,
In a race with time and sun.

A grain ship is lying at anchor,
There's a tugboat outward bound,
Overhead a jet is circling,
Waiting clearance from the ground.

Soon the rapture will be broken,
Time to rise and say adieu,
To the sunrise over the city,
Seattle, my love to you.

STRANGER NEVERMORE

On the island of Barbado's
I chanced to go ashore,
There I meet a stranger,
Now strangers nevermore.

I'm always a little nervous,
In new or distant lands,
Somehow you made me feel at home,
With smile and welcome hand.

Now we're strangers nevermore,
I'm very pleased to say,
I'll always remember meeting,
In a special heartfelt way.

A BAREFOOT BEACH

Barefoot is my favorite way,
When I'm adventure bound,
In search of hidden treasures,
On my beach in Puget Sound.

Guarded well by rugged cliffs,
You can only approach by sea,
Through a winding narrow channel,
A secret only known by few.

There I take my shoes off,
To walk barefoot and free,
Like a man of ancient times,
Where only God has majesty.

Gathering shells, stones, driftwood bones,
Treasures for my pack,
'Til it's time to say adieu,
To start my journey back.

Thank you God for another day,
Please accept the hand I reach,
In praise of all your majesty,
Thanks too for a barefoot beach.

TIME TO GO A SAILING

It's time to go a sailing,
Hear the morning breeze,
A boat is dancing at the dock,
Waiting for you and me.

Ah, to go a sailing,
Again, on the open sea,
Fresh winds and billowing sails,
White caps dancing free.

Come let's go a sailing,
Hurry down to the quay,
Where the blue water beckons,
Let's together spend the day.

It's time to go a sailing,
To have a wonderful day,
Thank the Gods for fair winds,
And then be on our way.

OCEANOGRAPHER FAREWELL

Aye, they say it is the time,
That you shall be no more,
Oh, gallant home upon the sea,
Many hearts will miss you sore.

Yet no tears will we shed,
Whatever shall be shall be,
Instead, we'll think of good times,
And the pleasant memories.

We'll think of all the good times,
Echoing still from other days,
Days of glory and excitement,
Since first you left the ways.

From your cruise of sixty-seven,
To the last in eighty-eight,
Of all the places visited,
Of sights both small and great.

We'll think of all the seamen,
Who gave their hearts to you,
Some of the ocean's finest,
Were proudly called your crew.

Aye, many a heart will miss you,
Many who loved and cared,
So, with that I'll say good-bye,
With an old salt's simple prayer.

Somewhere up in the heavens,
Where Gods are said to be,
I'm sending out an S.O.S.,
From all of us to thee.

And if it isn't possible,
Then fair winds and blue skies,
In our hearts you'll always be,
Where all good things lie.

BY THE SEA

Ere' the morning mist is rising,
You'll find me down by the shore,
In search of magic moments,
Memories to keep forever more.

There I walk where the past is gone,
By night tides washed away,
To greet the sunrise by the sea,
And welcome in the day.

Once more I'll watch the world awake,
Where the surf and seagulls vie,
Giving thanks to Mother Nature,
For a wonderful high.

WINTER TIDES

Only the bold and daring,
Venture forth on a wintery day,
In search of ocean treasures,
Winter tides bring their way.

Warmly bundled, parka and cap,
Oil skins and waterproof boots,
You'll find the lonely hunter,
In search of winter tide loot.

Glass balls, a fisherman's net,
Bottles from distant lands,
Driftwood carved and polished,
By surf and shifting sand.

A treasure trove such splendid view,
Soaring gulls and pounding surf,
The splendor of nature's beauty,
Where winter tides shape the earth.

THOUGHTS OF PLACES AND THINGS

FROM OTHER TIMES I'm thinking of thoughts, places, and things, some while I'm sleeping, others when awake. Long before the oceans beckoned, long before I heard the sirens sing. Of seasons, land, and people, and whatever thought my memory brings. My future is as, uncertain as my past, and I can only journey forward into the unknown.

INSCAPES

Inscapes are vivid pictures,
Life's impressions on the mind,
Painted there by humanities brush,
Both flattering and unkind.

Pathways to the future,
Or Hell, where all men lose,
What inscapes will the children have,
Each of us must choose.

Inscapes bright and beautiful,
Imprinted on a child's mind,
Painted by our example,
Children see and do in kind.

Each day I pray for wisdom,
To paint whatever I can,
Ever better than before,
Inscapes for future man.

TO YOURSELF

To yourself you must be true,
Keynote for a man's success,
Learn of strength and weakness,
Then strive your very best.

To yourself you owe it,
Don't ever settle for less,
Soon you'll see the wisdom,
Truth will always pass the test.

Success is at your fingertips,
You know what you must do,
Put your best foot forward,
And to yourself be true.

SUNSHINE EYES

Thank you, God for sunshine eyes,
They brighten up my days,
Bringing gladness to my heart,
As I travel along life's way.

I'm sure you made them special,
The one's with sunshine eyes,
To chase away the dark of gloom,
So, hope can once more rise.

Hope for all downtrodden,
Happiness for those alone,
Sunshine eyes are a blessing,
Wherever their brightness is shown.
So please keep them ever shining,
All my friends with sunshine eyes,
If possible, let me join in,
That I may too, bring blue skies.

TO LAUGH AGAIN

I must learn to laugh again,
As I did in days of yore,
'Ere the growing pains begin,
I did it so much more.

To laugh again as a little child,
Giggles of mirth, spontaneous, wild,
Vanquishing fears along the way,
As I walk this earthly mile.

I must learn to laugh again,
During times of trouble and strife,
To bring a smile where I can,
With laughter, the sweetest nectar of life.

To laugh again, a happy smile,
For all I chance to meet,
Laughter once again in style,
Joyous sounds on every street.
I must learn to laugh again,
Put a twinkle in my eye,
Laughter is a gift for man,
To keep his spirits high.

TO THOSE WHO DON'T GIVE IN

Standing up for what you believe,
Against what you feel is wrong,
Takes a lot of courage,
It's not easy to be strong.

There aren't too many people,
Who can take it on the chin,
Smile and keep going,
When it's easier to give in.

But there's a few, God bless 'em,
With guts to take a stand,
And though there isn't many,
They damn well deserve a hand.

It's good to have 'em by you,
Though you may not agree,
Knowing that they'll take a stand,
Is good enough for me.

I LOVE YOU

Fourth of July and fireworks,
Bursting loudly, sparkling bright,
Two lovers saying I love you,
Lending magic to the night.

Most beautiful of beautiful words,
I think I shall ever hear,
I love you whispered softly,
For someone I hold dear.

I remember days of childhood,
When mother tucked me in,
Good night my dear, I love you,
Always brought a happy grin.

I love you made a child well,
And chased the blues away,
Brought sunshine into a heart,
Upon a cloudy day.

I love you, words from Heaven,
I'm sure it must be so,
For whenever they are spoken,
My heart is set aglow.

Three little words, I love you,
Can light up the saddest face,
Don't be afraid to speak them,
Help make a happy face.

A CLOUDY SKY

I have a favorite grassy knoll,
Away from the hue and cry,
A very special place for me,
Where I watch the clouds roll by.

Pirate ships and treasure chests,
Old men with staffs of yew,
Dancing girls waving gaily,
All too, soon gone from view.

Kings and Queens, majestic thrones,
Picture stories in the sky,
Clouds are mighty battlefields,
Where knights and dragons vie.

Winged Pegasus for poets to ride,
Magic carpets on which to soar,
Watching clouds is all of this,
All of this and more.
For me a needed time of rest,
Relief from toil and strain,
Through the magic of a cloudy sky,
I feel refreshed again.

TOMORROW

I said I'll do it tomorrow,
But tomorrow never came,
I waited and I waited,
My wait was all in vain.

I'll do it, lost forever,
Vanished on tomorrow's wings,
For tomorrow never came,
It didn't bring a thing.

There's only now and yesterday,
Life and its memories,
I'll not wait for a tomorrow,
That I shall never see.

Today I'll store the memory,
Of a thousand yesterdays,
Tomorrow never happened,
It never came my way.

COUNTRY ROADS

I love to travel on country roads,
There's so many things of interest to me,
Majestic fields and rolling hills,
To lend a sense of dignity.

Each farm a little kingdom,
A certain air of majesty,
Around the bend a narrow road,
I expect a castle to see.

A kin to all I travel by,
Knight, errant, adventure bent,
At journey's end I'll salute my Lord,
Saying thanks for a day well spent.

COMPLIMENTS

Compliments are the flowers,
That light up a dreary day,
Compliments are the smiles,
In a world of disarray.

Compliments are encouragement,
When life has got you down,
Compliments are the wheels,
That can turn adversity around.
Compliments are the kindly acts,
That show another we care,
Compliments are born of love,
For all the world to share.

GENTLE HANDS

Gentle hands that touch me,
Born of love and care,
Upon my shelf of memories,
A special place is there.

Hands that held a puppy,
Gently stroked a kitten's fur,
The caring hands of doctors,
Searching for a cure.

Those of lovers touching,
Each sweet and gentle caress,
There upon my memory shelf,
Stand out above the rest.

Gentle hands a precious gift,
Given for me to see,
That I may gain in wisdom,
And in wisdom gentle be.

GRANDMA'S ROCKING CHAIR

Cleaning out the attic,
I came upon it there,
Covered by a dusty shawl,
Grandma's rocking chair.

Stirring memories of other days,
I could see her once again,
Gently rocking to and fro,
The same as she was then.

When little children got a hug,
Rocked in grandma's arms,
Snuggled closely to her breast,
Safely held from harm.

Her rocking chair is gone now,
Along with the dusty shawl,
To occupy a better place,
'Neath a picture on my wall.

A picture with a special smile,
When someone is sitting there,
Rocking a little one gently,
In Grandma's rocking chair.

ROSES

There's one last rose a blooming,
October is almost gone,
Falling leaves of autumn gold,
Dancing gaily across the lawn.

One last rose still waiting,
To grace a table fair,
The last of autumn's beauty,
Perhaps I should leave it there.
Nay, I think I shall pick it,
To tell someone I care,
That's why God made roses,
Exquisite beauty to share.

A CLOSING OF THE SEASON

FALL HAS ALWAYS held special meaning for me. It is a time of year when families gather, and often times, put their differences aside.

Starting with the children's laughter as they prepare for dress up, fun, and the chance to help the spirits along their way on All Hallows' Eve, better known to many as Halloween. Then to enjoy the few remaining tapestry colors of Autumn as they prepare to give thanks. Soon the quiet of winter will settle in, a time of reflection and solitude. Spring comes all too soon for one last stop at my favorite fishing hole. It is in these moments that I also continue on with the courage I will need to continue on life's difficult journeys. Then the ocean swells will once again beckon me, and back to days of sailing I'll go.

HALLOWEEN

Halloween, a time for haunting,
When all the fields are bare,
Black cats and witches all about,
Every shadow holds a scare.

Stories of spooks and goblins,
Are whispered in the night,
Children huddle close together,
By a jack-o-lantern light.

Haunted houses, trick or treat,
Halloween's a festive time,
At my door a little ghost,
Who must be home at nine.

And when the evening's over,
I say a little prayer,
Thanking God for Halloween,
A pleasant time to share.

AUTUMN

Glorious days of Indian summer,
Pageant of beauty by nature cast,
Over every field, hill and dale,
Autumn splendor, unsurpassed.

Scarlet, gold, and yellow hue,
A hunter's moon at night,
Jack-o-lanterns waiting in the field,
For home and candlelight.

Corn stalks add a ghostly view,
Visions of witches and such,
A time to count our blessings,
Autumn has given much.

THANKSGIVING

When the fields all are barren,
And trees like skeletons stand,
Their golden leaves a coverlet,
Upon the forest land.

There comes a time of solitude,
A time to reflect again,
When Jack Frost paints his murals
Across my windowpane.

To reflect on Spring and Summer,
Of a harvest safely stored,
Most hallowed time of blessing,
To thank a gracious Lord.

Time for friends and families,
To set aside their chores,
A time for love and worship,
At Grandma's house once more.

Of feasting and Thanksgiving,
With those that I hold dear,
A special feeling in my heart,
Thanksgiving time is here.

WINTER'S COMING

Autumn leaves are falling,
Time for earth to be abed,
A gold and yellow coverlet,
With generous splashes of red.

Squirrels wrapped in winter coats,
Snuggle in their nests,
The North wind sings a warning,
Of Winter's coming test.

The geese are flying southward,
I can hear them overhead,
Groundhogs are in their burrows,
Tucked into their beds.

A hushed excitement lingers,
Nature sings her lullaby,
Softly to the changes
Snow clouds are in the sky

SOLITUDE

There is a time in every life,
When we need to get away,
A time of quiet and solitude,
If only for a day.

A time to assess the future,
Review our hopes and plan,
Solitude should be a time,
To find ourselves again.

To me it is a treasure,
A time for me to find,
Strength to go another mile,
Rest for a weary mind.

A QUIET PLACE

I found myself a quiet place,
A little secluded glen,
Hidden away near a wilderness trail,
Apart from the world of men.

A place to escape a busy world,
When I feel my spirit wane,
There I drink from nature's well,
'Til once more I can maintain.

When I'm filled I thank her,
For the peace I'll carry within,
Say goodbye to my quiet place,
Then thank her once again.

MY FISHING HOLE

High up in a wilderness range,
There's a place I love to go,
A place of solitude and rest,
My favorite fishing hole.

Untouched, unspoiled by man's advance,
Mother nature's secret and mine,
Guarded well by bramble and thorn,
In a mountain glade sublime.

It's more than just a fishing hole,
But a place where I commune,
A time to be alone with nature,
And with nature keep in tune.

COURAGE

I'm found on every battlefield,
In every walk of life,
Within the heart of every man,
Through sickness and through strife.

Most never know I'm with them,
'Til old trouble comes around,
When disaster sets the drumbeat,
'Tis then I'm mostly found.

I am out upon the oceans,
Beneath the mastheads tall,
There midst the storms and tempest,
At every seaman's call.

With each boxer in the ring,
Each farmer in his fields,
Though bloody and beaten,
Never will I yield.

Now should you, God forbid it,
And feel that hope is gone,
I've been placed in every heart,
To help you carry on.

RAINBOW WARRIORS
(a tribute to Greenpeace)

Were I the greatest of poets,
This world has known by far,
I'd be hard pressed to tell,
Of all the things you are.

Your actions are all the people,
The one's we cannot see,
Who give so freely from their hearts,
People just like you and me.

Hearts with love of children,
God's creatures great and small,
A living tribute to the future,
Rainbow warriors one and all.

THE DEVIL'S PUNCHBOWL

A warning to all young sailormen,
With this I'm gonna tell,
I beg you pay attention,
Lest you find yourself in hell.

Aye, 'tis a tale of evil dark,
And of the devil's punchbowl,
Where down along the Oregon coast,
He's waiting for your soul.

Seems once he were a looking,
For a place where he cu'd brew,
Brew up a bunch of trouble,
Same as witches like to do.

He were a lookin' for a special place,
Wi' sailormen on his mind,
'Cause according to his tally,
He was laggin' far behind.

Sure enough one day he found it,
On a windswept rocky shore,
He found himself a perfect place,
To even up the score.

A punchbowl carved by nature,
Where havoc he cu'd brew,
By stirring up his evil schemes,
To sink good ships and crew.

Aye, to sink good ships and crew,
I know 'cause I were there,
My schooner tossed upon a rock,
Flotsam bobbing everywhere.

'Twas there I heard his laughter,
And knew the tale was true,
Of the devil and his punchbowl,
I swears by my tattoo.

STORYBOOK WAVES

A storybook wave came rolling in,
With a wonderous tale of the sea,
Of pirate ships and treasure chests,
Awaiting just for me.

Come away with me it said,
And be a spirit free,
Where riches are for taking,
In the wild Caribe.

To a fabled Treasure Island,
Where a scuttled Spainard lies,
There's chests of gold and silver,
A King's ransom for your eyes.

Now, storybook waves tell stories,
Just that and nothing more,
Still, I had to follow,
As a hundred times before.

For storybook waves and sirens,
Magic dragons and Honalee,
Are created by adventurous minds,
And old sea dogs like me.

COLLEEN
(with her talking eyes)

Were I a knight in shining amour,
With the world at my behest,
Should I meet with Colleen's eyes,
Other knights could have the rest.

Colleen, with her talking eyes,
That say so many things,
Unspoken words of tenderness,
Of wonderous love they sing.
Wonderous love for someone special,
A cup that overflows,
He who captures Colleen's heart,
Has found a pot of gold.

I'd gladly quit my wandering,
Give up my roving ways,
Should I find myself a Colleen,
With talking eyes one day..

THE PHANTOM BUCCANEERS

Once upon a sailing ship,
Beyond the portals of time,
Somewhere in a nether world,
Where shadows deceive your mind.

I were a bloody pirate captain,
With a wild blood thirsty crew,
An' if ye did'na lower yer colors,
We'd darn well run ya thru.

Perry Williams was me mate,
A devilish man of the sea,
The terror of the Spanish Main,
An' a whole lot meaner 'en me.

Onc't he cut a sailor's nose,
Jest for makin' a sneezing sound
Why e'en Black Beard gave wide berth,
When 'ol Perry were around.

Dutch Jack were the navigator,
A buccaneer of great renown,
For finding Spanish treasure ship,
An' even a few of The Crown.

Redbeard Waldo ran the crew,
A terrible man was he,
An' if ya gave him any lip,
It'd be shark feedin' time for ye.

Our crew they were a scurvy lot,
The worst in all the seas,
Handpicked by Redbeard Waldo,
Meanest ones ye ever did see.

We pillaged an' we plundered,
Throughout the Spanish Main,
So cussed and so ornery,

Folks were feared of our name.

That's why down thru history,
Ya never dare mention the name,
Of the dirtiest scurvy scumbags,
Whoever sailed the Main.
We were only known a phantoms,
A phantom ship and crew,
Who came to loot and plunder,
From somewhere outta the waves of blue

JAKE AND THE SEA BAG

I see'd 'em coming down a dock,
Like a clipper ship runnin' free,
Cap, salty, cocked upon his 'ead,
A weatherbeaten son a tha' sea.

Wi' his seabag on his shoulder,
A satchel in his hand,
Damned ol' Jake were comin' home,
From a sojourn on the land.

I remember well him a telling,
Last time he went ashore,
I'm putting my bag in a corner,
Ain't comin' out no more.

So it were I kinda' snickered,
When he tossed his gear aboard,
I suppose yer gonna tell me,
Ya gotta call from the Lord.

Well, it weren't exactly thataway,
But purty durn close sez he,
'Cause that there darned ol' seabag,
Started a talkin' back to me.

Jest a whining and a moanin',
'Til I couldn't take it no more,
'Bout how seabags and sailors,
Don't belong upon the shore.

I knows ya don't believe me,
But I swears 'tis gospel true,
I swears upon my sailor's cross,
As well as my tattoo.

When we clears the land's end,
That bags' going inta' the sea,
And when this voyage is over,

It's the last ye'll see of me.

Well sailors is as sailors are,
So, I sez to him,
Yer jest a durned ol' sea dog,
An' ye'll never pack it in.

Ya' better keeps the seabag,
'Cause yer never gonna be free,
As long as there are oceans,
That's where yer gonna be.

ABOUT THE AUTHOR

BORN IN 1926, Henry J. Jacobson, a streetwise tough from the wrong side of the tracks, fell in love with the ocean during WWII and has been going to sea ever since. Merchant seaman, tugboat man, fisherman, and oceanographer.

His second love came with his wife in the fifties. Though she bore him six children, it wasn't enough. The sea is a jealous mistress, and he could not refuse her call.

A seaman's life is a lonely life, a hard life for both the sailor and those he loves. Always a stranger are those who roam the seas until someday something happens and it becomes a love and hate affair. So, it was with his grandfather. The beauty of far-off romantic places has grown dim through the needs of a little child. Now to his grandfather, the seaman's life is just a job.

Having little wealth or possessions this book, and perhaps other writing efforts, is all he has to give as an inheritance. Should God and the spirit of the seas be willing he would like to spend his remaining time on earth writing poetry and getting to know his family. And just perhaps, have a little sloop so that he could share with them the beauty of his first love.

ABOUT THE ARTIST

Tonia J. Henry has always loved art and is passionate about creating in many forms. After taking every art class offered in grade school and winning several contests AND awards, she earned an Associate in Specialized Business with high honors (Alpha Society, President's Award, Dean's List) from Douglas Education Center, a Bachelor of Fine Arts/Minor in General Psychology with honors (Cum Laude, President's Honor Roll), and a Master of Arts in Illustration from Academy of Art University.

Inspired by the old masters as well as modern artists, she has experience in a variety of areas including traditional/digital painting and graphic design for narrative, editorial, and advertising projects. Artistically, she likes to mix mediums to create her distinctive style and enjoys working with subject matter ranging from figurative to floral and everything in between. Professionally, her work can be seen on military bases, book covers/illustrations, business logos, an array of products such as clothing and home goods, and framed in many homes.

An Air Force veteran, Tonia has authored four published books (pseudonym Talia Kendrix) and hosts a women's Healthy Boundaries self-care group to empower and encourage other survivors like her. For any/all inquiries, please feel free to reach out to her on the contact page of her website: https://toniahenry.wixsite.com/design.

www.ingramcontent.com/pod-product-compliance
Lightning Source LLC
Chambersburg PA
CBHW051630120626
46551CB00014B/2009

Empowering Self-Esteem for Young Girls *Building Confidence and Strength*

Empowering Self-Esteem for Young Girls *Building Confidence and Strength*

11 Inspiring Stories That Foster Self-Confidence for Teens and Encourage Growth Mindset

Aria Capri Publishing Group
Devon Abbruzzese
Mauricio Vasquez

Toronto, Canada

Authors:
Aria Capri Publishing Group
Devon Abbruzzese
Mauricio Vasquez

First Printing: December 2024

ISBN 978-1-998402-85-4 (Paperback)
ISBN 978-1-998402-86-1 (Hardcover)
ISBN 978-1-998402-87-8 (E-book)

To our daughter, Aria

You are the heart and inspiration behind every page of this book. Your courage, curiosity, and strength remind us daily why believing in ourselves is the greatest gift we can give.

Unlock More Inspiration for Your Teen!

Loved this book? There's more waiting for your daughter (and son)! Scan the QR code to explore:

- Uplifting stories and tools for building confidence.
- Workbooks to boost self-esteem and resilience.
- Exclusive tips for thriving in today's world.

💜 **Scan Now and keep the journey going!**

Join Our Exclusive Community

Ready to continue your journey beyond these pages? We'd love to connect. By joining our exclusive community, you'll:
- Get First Dibs on New Releases: Be the first to know about upcoming books and special projects.
- Access Exclusive Content & Perks: Enjoy behind-the-scenes insights, bonus resources, and priority invitations.
- Shape Future Works: Your feedback directly influences what we create next, making you part of the process.

Sound exciting? Scan the QR code. We can't wait to welcome you and share even more inspiration, guidance, and opportunities to grow—together!

Thanks for joining our exclusive circle, brought to you by Aria Capri Publishing, a company of MindScape Artwork!

Join Aria Capri Publishing on Patreon

Love the content so far? Stay even more connected with exclusive behind-the-scenes insights, patron-only perks, and sneak peeks of upcoming projects.

Simply scan this QR code (or follow the link) to become a patron and unlock a deeper level of engagement and support!

https://patreon.com/AriaCapriPublishing

Table of Contents

Introduction

Welcome to a collection of stories about courage, growth, and self-discovery. In these pages, you'll meet eleven young women, each navigating the challenges that come with figuring out who they are and where they belong. From academic pressure to fitting in, these characters face struggles that might feel familiar. But beyond the challenges, these stories offer something more: a journey toward building self-confidence and self-esteem.

Being a teenager can be tough. There's pressure to excel in school, keep up with trends, meet expectations, and fit into an ever-changing world. It's easy to feel like you're not enough or that you need to be perfect to be valued. But perfection is a myth, and your worth isn't tied to how you measure up against impossible standards. This book is here to remind you of that truth.

Each story in this collection explores a different challenge, but at their core, they all share the same message: confidence doesn't come from being flawless, and self-esteem isn't about seeking approval from others. Instead, it's about embracing your unique qualities, learning from your experiences, and realizing that you are worthy just as you are.

Through their journeys, the characters in this book discover that true confidence comes from within. They learn to navigate setbacks, face their fears, and celebrate their individuality. Whether it's finding strength after a stumble, embracing their creative passions, or learning to speak up, each character takes steps toward becoming their most authentic selves.

This book is for anyone who's ever felt unsure of themselves, who's doubted their abilities, or who's struggled to feel like they belong. It's for those who want to feel more confident in their own skin and believe in their worth.

As you read these stories, I hope you'll see reflections of your own experiences. I hope you'll feel inspired by these characters' resilience and reminded that confidence and self-esteem are built, not handed out. It's okay to make mistakes. It's okay to feel vulnerable. And it's more than okay to be exactly who you are.

So, let's begin. Together, let's explore the powerful, messy, and beautiful process of becoming your best, most confident self. The journey starts here.

<u>Share the Wisdom</u>

Dear Valued Reader,

Thank you for choosing this book to inspire confidence and growth in the teen girl in your life. Your feedback means so much to me and helps others discover these empowering stories.

As an independent author, your review plays a vital role in spreading this book's message. Simply scan the QR code below to share your thoughts—it only takes a moment but makes a big difference.

Your support means the world, and we are truly grateful.

With gratitude,

Devon & Mauricio

How to Use This Book

Welcome! You're holding a book that's more than just a collection of stories. It's a journey, a guide, and, hopefully, a friend that will help you navigate some of life's most challenging moments. Whether you're here to find inspiration, gain confidence, or simply connect with characters who feel as real as your own reflections, this book is designed to meet you where you are.

Start Where You Need

Each chapter in this book introduces a different character, facing challenges that might feel familiar to you. From dealing with perfectionism to struggling with self-expression, every story touches on themes of resilience, self-confidence, and self-esteem. You don't need to read the stories in order; think of this book as a toolbox. Start with the story that speaks to you most, whether it's about overcoming fear of failure, embracing your individuality, or finding balance in your life.

Reflect and Relate

After each story, take a moment to reflect. Ask yourself:

- **What parts of this story resonate with me?**
- **Have I faced similar challenges? How did I respond?**
- **What can I learn from the character's journey?**

You'll notice that the characters often have internal monologues that reflect their thoughts and emotions. Use these moments to connect with your own feelings. You might even want to jot down your thoughts in a journal. Consider writing about your own experiences, victories, or even the things that still feel like struggles. There's power in putting your thoughts into words.

Take Small Steps

The lessons in this book aren't about making grand changes overnight. Instead, they're about recognizing small, meaningful shifts. Perhaps one story inspires you to speak up a little more in class. Another might encourage you to take a break when you're feeling overwhelmed. Each step, no matter how small, brings you closer to embracing your unique strengths and growing your confidence.

Use the Pause Moments

Throughout the book, you'll find moments where the characters pause to reflect, often through an internal thought or a conversation with a mentor. These are your prompts to pause, too. Think about what advice you would give to a friend in a similar situation—or what advice you'd like to hear for yourself. This book is as much about learning from others as it is about learning from within.

Share and Discuss

Sometimes, the best way to understand something is by sharing it. If a particular story moves you, talk about it with a friend, parent, or teacher. Sharing your thoughts can spark meaningful conversations and help you see that you're not alone in your experiences.

Be Kind to Yourself

This book is about embracing who you are, imperfections and all. As you read, remember: growth isn't linear, and it's okay to have setbacks. The characters in these stories don't achieve their breakthroughs in a single moment—they stumble, they reflect, and they rise again. Allow yourself the same grace.

A Journey for Today—and Tomorrow

You might find yourself coming back to this book at different points in your life. What resonates today might feel different a few months or years from now. That's the beauty of growth—it's ongoing. Let this book be a companion on your journey, reminding you that every challenge is an opportunity to learn, and every setback is a chance to rise.

Final Thoughts

You are capable of incredible things. This book is here to remind you of that. Each story is a mirror, reflecting the strength, courage, and resilience that already exist within you. Take your time, be patient with yourself, and remember: your worth isn't defined by achievements or external validation. It's found in the way you embrace your true self, every single day.

Now, let's begin. Your journey awaits.

Story 1 - Finding Her Voice

Aria stood in front of the mirror, her reflection staring back at her with a critical eye. Her fingers fidgeted with the edge of her sweater, a deep blue that was supposed to bring out her eyes but today felt like it highlighted all the wrong things.

No matter how hard she tried, she couldn't see anything good in what the mirror showed her. The more she looked, the more flaws seemed to appear—her hair, which never seemed to fall the right way; her skin, which wasn't as clear as she wished; and her figure, which she constantly compared to the other girls at school.

"Why can't I just look like them?" she thought, her heart sinking. In her mind, there was always a comparison, always a way she fell short. She pulled her hair into a tight ponytail, hoping to look presentable. But even as she left her room, the doubts followed her like a shadow.

At school, the feeling of inadequacy grew heavier with each step down the crowded hallway. Aria kept her gaze fixed on the floor, avoiding the glances of her classmates. She could hear the laughter of the popular girls as they passed, their confidence and beauty so effortlessly on display. Aria felt invisible, and she preferred it that way. Being noticed meant being judged, and she had enough judgment in her own head without adding anyone else's opinions to the mix.

The day dragged on, a blur of classes and quiet anxiety. By the time the final bell rang, she was exhausted from the mental battle she fought every day. But something different was waiting for her as she entered the auditorium for the school assembly. The principal's voice echoed through the large room, announcing the upcoming talent show. For a moment, Aria's heart skipped a beat.

Singing had always been her secret passion, a way to escape the constant self-doubt, but the thought of performing in front of others made her stomach twist with fear.

"Only the prettiest and most talented should even try." Jenna's voice rang out, cutting through the murmur of the crowd. Her words hit Aria like a punch to the gut. *"She's right,"* Aria thought, the brief flicker of hope extinguished as quickly as it had appeared. *"There's no way I could ever do that"*.

After the assembly, Aria found herself standing in front of the talent show sign-up sheet, her hand hovering over the pen. The hallway was nearly empty, but the weight of the decision felt overwhelming. Could she really put herself out there and risk being seen and judged? The doubts crowded her mind, and with a heavy sigh, she turned away, her heart heavy with disappointment and relief. She had let fear win, once again choosing the safety of invisibility over the risk of rejection.

Later, in the quiet of the music room, Aria sat alone at the piano. her fingers tracing the keys but not pressing down. The room felt like the only place where she could be herself, away from the pressures and judgments of the outside world. She didn't even notice when Ms. Harper, the music teacher, entered.

"You have a beautiful voice, Aria." Ms. Harper said, her voice warm and kind. *"I've heard you sing when you think no one is listening."*

Aria looked up, surprised. *"But I'm not good enough,"* she mumbled, the familiar doubts rising to the surface. *"I'm not like the other girls. I can't..."*

"Aria, your voice is unique, just like you." Ms. Harper interrupted gently. *"It doesn't matter what anyone else thinks. What matters is how you feel when you sing. Do you love it?"*

Aria hesitated, then nodded slowly. *"I do,"* she admitted, her voice barely a whisper. *"But..."*

"No buts," Ms. Harper smiled. *"Don't let fear stop you from doing what you love. The world needs to hear your voice."*

As she left the music room, Ms. Harper's words echoed in Aria's mind. For the first time in a long while, she felt a flicker of hope. Maybe—just maybe—she could find the courage to step out of the shadows. But the doubts were still there, lurking in the corners of her mind, waiting for the right moment to drag her back down.

Aria's heart pounded in her chest as she stood in front of the sign-up sheet once again. The hallway was empty, but her mind was crowded with the echoes of doubt that had held her back the first time. She stared at the blank lines, the pen trembling in her hand. A small voice inside her urged her to walk away, to stay safe in the comfort of invisibility. But Ms. Harper's words kept replaying in her mind: *"Your voice is a gift. Don't let fear stop you from doing what you love."*

Taking a deep breath, Aria forced her hand to steady and quickly scrawled her name on the list. It wasn't neat and it wasn't perfect, but it was there—her first step toward something new, something terrifying. The weight of the pen felt heavier than she had expected, as if signing her name was not just a commitment to perform but a commitment to herself.

As soon as she finished, a rush of anxiety washed over her. *"What have I done?"* she thought, her heart racing. She could almost hear the whispers of her classmates, the judgmental looks, the snickers behind her back. The fear was nearly paralyzing, but mixed in with that fear was a tiny flicker of something else—something like pride. For once, she hadn't let the fear win.

The days leading up to the talent show were a blur of rehearsals and quiet panic. Every time she stood on the stage for practice, she felt exposed, vulnerable, as if every eye in the room was focused on her flaws. The first time she sang, her voice was shaky, and she could barely meet Ms. Harper's encouraging gaze.

"Try again, Aria." Ms. Harper said gently, her voice a calm anchor in the storm of Aria's nerves. *"Close your eyes if you need to, but remember why you're here."*

Aria nodded, taking a deep breath. She closed her eyes, shutting out the empty seats and the overwhelming fear of failure. As she sang, something shifted within her. For a moment, it wasn't about how she looked or how others would judge her—it was about the music, about expressing something she couldn't quite put into words.

When she finished, Ms. Harper smiled, a look of quiet pride in her eyes. *"That's the Aria I know."* she said. *"You're stronger than you think."*

But even with Ms. Harper's support, the doubts lingered. As the talent show drew closer, the tension inside Aria tightened like a coiled spring. Every morning, she stared into the mirror, her old insecurities rearing their heads again. She would see the imperfections, the flaws she couldn't hide, and wonder if she was making a mistake by putting herself out there.

The night before the talent show, Aria sat on her bed, staring at the sheet music in her lap. Her hands shook as she traced the notes on the page, the familiar melody feeling foreign under the weight of her anxiety. *"What if I fail? What if I stood on that stage and all I saw were the judging eyes of her peers?"*

"You're unique, Aria. And that's your strength." Ms. Harper's words echoed in her mind, a lifeline in the swirling sea of doubt.

With a shaky breath, Aria set the music aside and closed her eyes. She pictured herself on the stage, but this time, instead of seeing the faces of others, she imagined herself singing alone, just for herself. For the first time, she let herself believe that maybe—just maybe—this wasn't about proving something to the world. Maybe it was about proving something to herself.

The thought was both terrifying and liberating. Aria opened her eyes, a new resolve hardening in her chest. Tomorrow, she would take the stage. Not for them, but for her. And maybe, just maybe, that would be enough.

The next day arrived like a wave of anticipation, crashing into the pit of Aria's stomach. She could barely focus through her morning classes, her mind wandering to the stage that awaited her. As the school day wore on, the chatter of her peers buzzed around her, but Aria was distant, her thoughts swirling with the lines of her song. By the time the final bell rang, the weight of what was to come felt both heavier and lighter. This was her moment.

When she stepped into the auditorium, the lights were dim, and the soft hum of conversations filled the air. Her palms were damp, and her heart raced in time with the clock ticking, counting down to her performance. As she waited backstage, Aria inhaled deeply, the sounds of other performances barely registering as she mentally rehearsed her piece. She could feel her heart pounding in her chest, but with each beat, she reminded herself why she was doing this—not for them, but for her.

The final note of Aria's song hung in the air, echoing through the auditorium like a whispered promise. For a heartbeat, there was silence, the kind that swells before something big happens. Aria stood on the stage, her heart pounding, eyes still closed as if she could hold onto the safety of that moment just a little longer.

Then, the applause began. It started softly, like a tentative ripple, then grew into a wave that crashed over her, filling the room with a warmth that took her breath away. Aria opened her eyes, blinking in disbelief at the faces turned toward her, all of them smiling, clapping, not judging, not laughing—just appreciating.

She had done it. The realization hit her like a burst of sunlight after a long, stormy night. She had faced her fears, stood in the spotlight, and let herself be seen—not as the girl who always tried to hide, but as someone who had something worth sharing. And they had seen her, really seen her, for who she was.

Ms. Harper stood at the edge of the stage, her eyes shining with pride. Aria met her gaze, and for the first time, she didn't look away in embarrassment or doubt. Instead, she smiled—a real, unguarded smile.

"I knew you could do it." Ms. Harper said softly as Aria stepped off the stage, the applause still ringing in her ears.

Aria's smile widened, the weight of her old insecurities lifting, piece by piece. *"I wasn't sure I could."* she admitted, her voice steady despite the whirlwind of emotions inside her. *"But once I started singing, it wasn't about them anymore. It was about me, and what I love."*

Ms. Harper nodded, a knowing look in her eyes. *"That's the secret, Aria. It's always been about you embracing who you are, not what others see."*

As Aria walked through the crowded hallway the next morning, the familiar buzz of student chatter surrounded her. But this time, the sounds didn't feel overwhelming. She didn't keep her eyes on the floor or try to disappear into the background. Instead, she walked with her head held high, meeting the gazes of those around her with a quiet confidence she had never felt before.

"Hey, Aria!" someone called out. She turned to see Mia, one of the quieter girls in her class, hurrying to catch up with her. *"That was amazing last night! I never knew you could sing like that."*

Aria felt a warmth spread through her chest, not just at the compliment, but at the realization that she wasn't invisible anymore—and she was okay with that. *"Thanks, Mia,"* she said, her voice filled with genuine appreciation. *"It felt good to finally share it."*

Mia smiled, a hint of shyness in her expression. *"I wish I could be that brave."*

Aria paused, considering her words carefully. *"You know."* she began, *"I didn't think I was brave either. I was terrified. But sometimes, being brave isn't about not being scared. It's about doing something anyway, because it's important to you."*

Mia looked thoughtful, and Aria could see the spark of hope in her eyes—the same spark Ms. Harper had ignited in her not so long ago. *"Maybe... maybe I'll try something like that someday."*

Aria nodded, feeling a new sense of purpose blooming within her. *"And when you do, I'll be there to cheer you on."*

As Mia walked away, Aria stood in the hallway for a moment, letting the weight of everything that had happened sink in. She wasn't the same girl who had tried to fade into the background at the beginning of the year. She had changed, and grown, not just in how she saw herself, but in how she saw the world around her.

The hallway, once filled with obstacles and fears, now seemed open and full of possibilities. Aria took a deep breath, feeling the steady beat of her heart, and knew that she had finally come home—not just to the school, but to herself.

Learning Lessons from "Finding Her Voice"

Aria's journey shows you the power of vulnerability and self-expression, even when self-doubt feels overwhelming. Courage isn't about being fearless—it's about taking action despite the fear. By choosing to share her voice, even when she felt uncertain and imperfect, Aria reveals an important truth: your unique strengths shine brightest when you embrace who you truly are.

Her story reminds you not to compare yourself to others, because doing so only steals your joy. Trying to measure up to someone else's standards will never let you see your own worth. Instead, self-worth comes from valuing yourself for who you are, not for how others perceive you.

Aria's experience also highlights the importance of having people in your corner—like Ms. Harper, whose encouragement helped Aria step outside her comfort zone. Sometimes, the right words from someone who believes in you can give you the strength to try something new.

Most importantly, Aria's bravery inspires others, showing that when you take the first step, you can light the way for someone else. Your courage has the power to ripple outward, helping others find their own strength.

You have a voice that's worth hearing, and when you let yourself be seen, you might discover a confidence you never thought possible.

Story 2 - More Than Enough

The early morning sunlight filtered through the blinds, casting soft lines across Lila's bedroom. She blinked her eyes open, the familiar weight settling in her chest even before her feet touched the floor. Her hand instinctively reached for her phone, fingers brushing against its cool surface.

"Another day. Another reminder of everything I wasn't" Lila thought as she opened Instagram, her thumb swiping up the screen almost automatically. Perfect faces. Flawless skin. Laughing, shining girls, their hair catching the light just right. Lila's gaze lingered on a photo of a girl her age, her heart sinking.

"Why can't I look like that?" she wondered, her stomach tightening.

She knew the influencer in the picture didn't really look like that—not all the time, anyway—but it didn't matter. All she saw was perfection. Every swipe made her more invisible, more insignificant, as if the bright, edited photos on her screen were draining the color from her own world. She touched her face, fingers tracing over a pimple near her chin. Her skin never seemed to cooperate.

With a heavy sigh, Lila tossed her phone onto her bed and crossed the room to the mirror. The reflection staring back at her felt like a stranger—someone trapped between wanting to disappear and wishing she could be noticed.

"*Why do I always feel like I'm not enough?*" The question whispered through her mind like a quiet echo, one she couldn't seem to shake.

"*I'm never going to look like them.*" Her eyes traced the curve of her cheeks, the freckles dotting her nose. "*No matter what I do, there's always something wrong.*"

The longer she stared, the more flaws she found—her eyebrows uneven, her hair refusing to lie flat, her body too soft in all the wrong places. The weight of it all pressed down on her, making her want to crawl back under the covers and hide from the world.

It wasn't just the photos on her feed—it was the constant reminder that everyone else seemed to have figured it out. The perfect skin, the tiny waists, the effortless confidence. And then there was her. Always feeling like she was falling short. Always feeling like if she just tried a little harder, maybe she'd feel better about herself. Maybe then, people would see her.

But it never seemed to be enough. No matter how many beauty tips she tried, no matter how many selfies she deleted because they didn't live up to the standards she had built in her mind, the nagging voice of doubt never went away.

A soft knock sounded on her door. "*Lila?*" It was her older sister, Maya, peeking her head in. "*You alright? You've been in here a while.*"

Lila quickly swiped at her eyes, hoping Maya hadn't noticed. "*Yeah, just... looking at stuff.*"

Maya stepped into the room, glancing at the phone on Lila's bed and the mirror where Lila stood. She didn't have to ask to know what was going through her sister's mind. Maya had been there before.

"You know..." Maya began gently, sitting on the edge of Lila's bed, "*I used to spend hours staring at my phone, comparing myself to people online. I thought if I could just change one thing, I'd finally be happy.*"

Lila glanced over at her sister, her throat tight. "*And did it work?*"

Maya smiled, a soft, understanding smile. "*Not at all. I realized that I was chasing something that wasn't even real. Most of the time, those pictures are edited, and even if they're not, they only show the parts people want you to see. You're comparing yourself to an illusion.*"

Maya said softly "*You're so much more than what you see on that screen, Lila. You've got this amazing smile and such a big heart. You can't measure your worth by someone else's highlight reel.*"

Lila sat down next to Maya, her mind racing. "*Could it really be that simple? That the problem wasn't me?*" she wondered. She wanted to believe it. Wanted to think that she didn't have to change to be accepted. But the doubts clung to her like a second skin.

"*But how do I stop feeling like this? How do I stop comparing myself to them when it's everywhere I look?*"

Maya reached out, gently tilting Lila's chin so she was looking into her eyes. "*It starts with believing that you are enough, exactly as you are. No filter, no edits. Just you.*"

As Maya left the room, Lila felt the weight of her phone calling to her from the bed. It would be so easy to fall back into the habit—scrolling, comparing, and feeling less than. But for the first time in a long while, she felt a small flicker of hope. "*Maybe Maya was right.*" she thought. "*Maybe there was more to me than I'd been willing to see.*"

Lila walked back to the mirror, the girl in the reflection still looking unsure, still feeling like she had a long way to go. But now, she saw something else too—a quiet strength she hadn't noticed before. And while she wasn't sure if she believed everything Maya had said, she was willing to try.

For the first time that morning, Lila turned away from the mirror and left her phone on the bed. She wasn't sure what would come next, but maybe that was okay. Maybe figuring it out was part of the journey.

The next day, the familiar clang of lockers and chatter of students filled the air as Lila made her way through the crowded school halls. The bustle of the school day surrounded her, but it felt distant, almost muted, as she walked to her classroom. By the time she sat down at her desk, her thoughts were still tangled with the conversation she'd had with Maya.

Lila sat at her desk, staring at the blank notebook in front of her. The low hum of voices drifted from the school hallway, but she was lost in her own thoughts, running over the conversation with Maya again and again.

"*You're comparing yourself to an illusion.*" Maya had said. It had sounded simple when she said it, but letting go of those comparisons wasn't easy, especially when it felt like every glance at her phone pulled her back into the same trap—an endless loop of judgment and inadequacy.

Her eyes flicked to her phone, its screen dark on the desk, like a silent challenge.

"*What if I never feel like I'm enough? What if this feeling doesn't go away, no matter what I do?*" she questioned herself.

The thought settled heavily in her chest. She looked around the classroom at the other girls, some laughing, others scrolling through their phones. Every movement seemed effortless, as if they weren't carrying the same weight that she was. They looked so sure of themselves, so comfortable in their skin. Lila tugged at her sleeve, pulling it down to cover her wrists, as if hiding part of herself would make her invisible.

Just then, the classroom door opened, and the teacher walked in, her voice breaking through Lila's haze. "*Alright, everyone, put your phones away. I have a project I'm assigning today.*"

Lila barely listened as the teacher explained, something about creating a personal project that showcased their strengths—something unique about each student. But when the teacher mentioned that each project would be presented at the school's annual talent showcase, Lila's stomach tightened. The thought of putting herself out there for everyone to see made her palms sweat.

The teacher continued. *"Think about what makes you. What are you passionate about? What's something that makes you unique?"*

Lila's thoughts spiraled. *"What if I don't have anything that makes me unique? What if I'm just... ordinary?"* The word stung in her mind, leaving an ache behind it. She'd spent so long trying to fit into the mold, trying to look like everyone else, that she didn't even know where to start.

She turned the pencil over in her hands, chewing on the edge of the eraser as her mind swirled with doubts.

Later that afternoon, Lila found herself in the kitchen, slumped at the counter, idly scrolling through her phone again—against her better judgment. She hadn't even realized she was doing it until Maya walked in. Lila quickly locked her phone and placed it face down on the counter, as if the act itself would somehow erase the guilt she felt.

Maya raised an eyebrow but said nothing. Instead, she placed a cup of tea next to Lila and leaned against the counter. *"You look like something's on your mind."*

Lila sighed. *"We got this project today, and we're supposed to show what makes us unique, something we're passionate about, but I have no idea what to do. Everyone else seems to know who they are, but I... don't."*

Maya frowned thoughtfully and then smiled. *"You've always had this amazing way with words. I've seen the poems you've written—why not start there?"*

Lila hesitated. *"My poems? But... I've never shared them with anyone. They're just for me."*

Maya smiled gently. "Exactly. They're yours. That's what makes them special. Writing is how you see the world. Maybe it's time you shared that with others."

Lila hesitated. The idea of letting people see that part of her felt raw and vulnerable, but there was something about the way Maya said it— like it was a gift, not something to be ashamed of.

That night, Lila sat at her desk again, the same blank notebook in front of her. This time, she flipped to the back pages where she had scribbled poems over the last year. She ran her fingers over the words, reading over the quiet, secret thoughts she had never let anyone see.

"Maybe this is who I am. Maybe this is what makes me unique." She swallowed hard, feeling the flutter of nerves in her stomach, but also something else—something lighter. Hope.

Lila picked up her pencil and began to write again, not for herself this time, but with the intention of sharing her words with the world. She didn't know how people would react, and that uncertainty still scared her. But for the first time, it didn't matter as much. What mattered was that she was doing something for *her*, something real and honest.

A week later, the school's annual talent showcase approached faster than she expected. The event was now a reality, no longer just a distant thought. With every passing day, Lila found herself rehearsing, scribbling new lines, and reading her poems aloud in the quiet of her room. Her nerves grew as the performance day neared, but this time, she felt a flicker of determination alongside the anxiety.

On the day of the event, she stood behind the curtain, waiting for her name to be called. Her hands trembled slightly, but there was no turning back. This was her moment.

Lila stood on the edge of the stage, her heart pounding in her chest as she scanned the sea of faces staring back at her. The lights were warm, almost too bright, and the hum of the crowded auditorium buzzed in her ears. The school's talent showcase had always been something she avoided—a place where students stood under the spotlight, judged not only by their abilities but also by how perfectly they could present themselves.

This year was different.

In her hands, she clutched a small notebook, worn from being flipped through too many times, the pages soft and folded at the corners. It was her poetry journal. The one Maya had encouraged her to share, the one that had been her private refuge for so long. But now, it was her voice.

"*I can't believe I'm actually doing this.*" Lila's breath came faster, her nerves tightening with every passing second. "*What if they don't get it? What if they laugh?*"

Her mind flashed back to all the times she had stood in front of the mirror, scrutinizing every detail, wishing she could hide her imperfections. She thought about how she had hidden parts of herself—her thoughts, her voice, her body—hoping it would make her fit in, make her more acceptable.

But the truth was, she was done with hiding.

"*I've spent so much time trying to be someone I'm not.*" she thought, gripping the edges of the notebook tighter. "*This is me. This is what I have to offer.*"

The murmurs from the audience faded as the teacher introduced her. "*Next, we have Lila Jones, who will be sharing her original poetry.*"

Lila swallowed hard, feeling every pair of eyes turn to her. This was it. No filters. No edits. Just her, standing in front of her peers, vulnerable and real. She could feel her hands trembling slightly, but she wasn't turning back now.

She thought of Maya's words, echoing in her mind like a gentle reminder.

"*Your words matter, Lila. You matter. Don't be afraid to show the world who you really are.*"

It was that final push she needed. Lila took a deep breath, stepping into the center of the stage. Her heart raced, but as she looked down at her notebook, the familiar words staring back at her, something inside her steadied.

The first line of her poem escaped her lips quietly, her voice uncertain at first, but growing stronger with each word. This time, she wasn't holding back. Lila shared the whole poem, the one she had written not just for herself, but for anyone who had ever felt small, unseen, or not enough:

> *"We are more than what the mirror shows,*
> *More than the likes, the comments, the clothes.*
> *We are the stories we hold deep inside,*
> *The fears we face, the tears we've cried.*
>
> *We are the dreams we keep in our hearts,*
> *The quiet strengths that set us apart.*
> *Not defined by the standards they create,*
> *But by the courage to challenge our fate.*
>
> *We are more than what they say we should be,*
> *More than the filters that blur what they see.*
> *We are the voices that rise and stand tall,*
> *Unique in our beauty, enough through it all."*

She could hear her voice resonate across the room, filling the silence. The vulnerability in her words hung in the air, palpable. But with each stanza, she felt herself standing a little taller, her voice becoming steadier.

As she recited the last lines, she realized something: she wasn't scared anymore. She wasn't performing for their approval. She was sharing a piece of herself—her truth—and it didn't matter how they reacted.

"For so long, I thought I had to be perfect. But this, right here, is what's real. This is me."

A calm washed over her, and for the first time in a long time, Lila felt free. She wasn't hiding behind an image, a filter, or anyone's expectations. She was standing in her own truth, and that was enough.

The auditorium was still for a moment when she finished. Then, slowly, applause began to build. At first, it was polite, but it grew louder, stronger. Lila blinked, looking out at the faces in the crowd. Some looked surprised, others inspired. But most of all, they weren't laughing. They weren't judging her. They were just... listening.

"They're listening to me." Lila thought, her heart swelling with pride. *"Not for how I look, but for what I have to say."*

As she stepped down from the stage, Maya was waiting for her at the side, beaming. *"You were amazing, Lila."*

Lila smiled, a real smile this time. *"Thanks. It felt... good."* She exhaled slowly, feeling the tension melt away. *"Really good."*

Maya smiled, her eyes filled with pride. *"See? I told you, Lila. You've always had this in you."*

Lila looked back at the stage, then at her sister. She had crossed a threshold tonight, not just with her poetry, but with herself. She had returned to the world, not as the insecure girl who doubted every inch of her body or her worth, but as someone who finally believed in her own voice, her own beauty.

Lila then declared to the world, *"This is me. I'm not perfect, but I'm more than enough. I've always been more than enough."*

Learning Lessons from "More Than Enough"

Lila's story is a reminder that your worth is not defined by what you see on a screen or in a mirror. It's easy to get caught up in comparisons and believe you need to change to be accepted, but true beauty lies in being authentically you. The filtered perfection on social media is not real life, and chasing it will only leave you feeling empty. Instead, focus on what makes you unique—your passions, your kindness, and your voice.

Maya's wisdom to Lila highlights an important truth: self-acceptance begins with letting go of the need to measure up to others. You don't need to change to be enough—you already are. Every freckle, every flaw, every strength and struggle is part of the person only you can be.

Lila's courage to share her poetry teaches that vulnerability is a strength, not a weakness. When you let others see the real you, you create connections and inspire those around you. The applause Lila received wasn't for being perfect—it was for being brave, real, and true to herself.

Remember, your voice matters. Your uniqueness is your power. And no matter what the world says, you are more than enough—always have been, always will be.

Story 3 - Sketching Strength

The morning light filtered through the half-drawn blinds of Ava's room, casting soft shadows on the familiar space around her. She lay still in bed, staring through the window. There was a weight in her chest, that dull ache she'd grown used to. She sighed, pulling the blankets tighter around herself as if they could shield her from the outside world.

Her phone buzzed on the nightstand, and instinctively, she reached for it, her fingers tracing the cool glass of the screen. Social media was a ritual—one she didn't particularly enjoy but couldn't seem to quit either. Her thumb scrolled absently, passing perfectly curated photos of classmates, their smiling faces a cruel contrast to how she felt inside.

"Why do they make it look so easy?" Ava thought, a familiar knot tightening in her stomach. *"How do they always look so... put together?"*

She stopped at a picture of a group of girls from her school, their flawless outfits and glowing skin glowing back at her. They looked so confident, so carefree. Ava's eyes darted to the reflection in her mirror across the room, and she felt her heart sink. Baggy hoodie, messy hair, and dark circles under her eyes from a sleepless night. It was like looking at a stranger. She avoided the mirror whenever possible—something about it made her want to hide.

At school, the day unfolded like any other. Ava sat quietly at the back of the classroom, her notebook open but untouched. The hum of chatter from her classmates filled the room, but Ava felt disconnected, like an outsider looking in.

Her teacher's voice cut through the noise. "Alright, class. We're starting a new project—something that's all about you. I want each of you to create something that represents who you are, something unique to you."

Ava's pulse quickened. *"Something that represents me?"* Her mind raced. *"What do I have to show?"*

The words stirred something inside her—a mix of curiosity and fear. The idea of creating something personal terrified her. She wasn't like the other girls. She didn't have that effortless confidence, the kind that made people notice her for all the right reasons.

As the class ended, Ava gathered her things and bolted for the door, trying to ignore the rising panic in her chest. *"I can't do this"*, she thought, her fingers gripping the straps of her backpack tightly as she navigated the crowded hallway. *"I don't even know who I am, let alone what makes me special"*.

For the rest of the day, Ava found herself trapped in a loop of self-doubt. Whenever she thought about the project, her mind filled with images of her classmates—beautiful, confident, unbothered. And then there was her: ordinary, invisible, unsure.

Later, in the safety of her bedroom, Ava paced the floor, frustration bubbling up. She hated this feeling of inadequacy, but it clung to her like a shadow. She wanted to ignore the assignment, pretend it didn't matter. But deep down, the idea of letting everyone see how lost she really felt scared her even more.

A soft knock came from her door. *"Ava?"* It was Zoe, her older cousin, who had come to stay for a few weeks. Ava hesitated but opened the door, allowing Zoe into the room.

Zoe was the opposite of Ava—bold, vibrant, and unapologetically herself. Ava had always admired her, but she also felt jealous whenever Zoe seemed so comfortable in her skin. Today, though, there was a different energy in the room. Zoe sat down beside her, reading the heaviness in Ava's expression.

"What's going on, kiddo?" Zoe asked gently, her voice full of warmth.

Ava didn't know how to put it into words at first. *"We got this project at school."* she mumbled. *"Something about showing who we are, but... I don't think I can do it."*

Zoe raised an eyebrow, intrigued. *"Why not?"*

Ava looked down at her hands. *"Because I don't know who I am. I'm... I'm nothing special. I don't have that confidence like you. I don't have anything worth showing."*

Zoe smiled softly, leaning forward. *"I used to think the same thing. But let me tell you something: Confidence doesn't come from trying to be like everyone else. It comes from learning to accept what makes you different. You've got so much more going on than you give yourself credit for, Ava."*

Ava frowned, not sure she believed it. *"But... what if they don't like what they see? What if I'm just... ordinary?"*

Zoe placed a hand on Ava's shoulder. *"Trust me, kid. You are far from ordinary. It's time you start seeing that."*

That night, Ava lay in bed, her mind buzzing. Zoe's words echoed in her head: *"It's time you start seeing that"*. Could it really be that simple? That maybe she had something to offer, something worth showing?

She tossed and turned, wrestling with the idea. She could play it safe, hand in something generic, and continue hiding behind the walls she'd built around herself. Or, she could take a risk—just once—by stepping into the spotlight.

The thought was terrifying, but a small flicker of hope tugged at her. Ava sat up in bed, pulling her sketchbook out from beneath her pillow. Slowly, hesitantly, she began to draw.

Maybe, she thought, as the lines formed beneath her pencil, *"Maybe there's more to me than I've been willing to see"*

She wasn't sure where this journey would lead, but for the first time, she was willing to take the first step.

The next morning, Ava walked into school with her sketchbook clutched tightly under her arm. The familiar hum of students moving through the halls filled the air, lockers slamming shut, and laughter echoing from groups of friends. She kept her head down, navigating the crowded hallway until she found her usual spot in the cafeteria, tucked away near the back where she could be alone.

The soft buzz of voices filled the cafeteria, but Ava barely heard any of it. Her focus was on the sketchbook sitting in her lap, open to the drawing she had been working on for her school project. She had spent hours the previous night sketching—pouring her insecurities, her hopes, and her fears into the art. But now, in the harsh light of day, her confidence was unraveling.

"What if it's not good enough?" The familiar doubt crept in. Ava glanced around the cafeteria at her classmates, who seemed so at ease in their own skin, laughing and talking without care. And then, there were the girls she avoided—the ones who had made a habit of commenting on her clothes, her body, her everything.

Her stomach turned as she spotted them across the room. Instinctively, she pulled her hoodie tighter around herself, as if it could shield her from their gaze. She didn't want to draw attention, but one of the girls caught her eye and smirked.

"*Still trying to hide under that hoodie, Ava?*" the girl called out, loud enough for the surrounding tables to hear... "*It's not working.*"

Laughter echoed around her, each chuckle like a sharp pin pricking at her confidence. Ava's heart pounded, and for a moment, she felt the crushing weight of self-doubt threatening to suffocate her. "*Why can't I be like them? Why am I always the target?*

Before Ava could retreat into herself, she felt a presence beside her. It was Clara, her friend who had always been quietly supportive, but never outspoken. Today was different.

"*Leave her alone!*" Clara said, her voice steady and firm. The laughter died down, and the cafeteria noise resumed. The bullies, now uninterested, turned their attention elsewhere.

Ava blinked in surprise, her heart still racing. "*You didn't have to do that*" she murmured, feeling embarrassed by the attention.

"*I know*" Clara replied, giving Ava a small smile. "*But you shouldn't have to deal with them alone.*"

The words hit Ava deeper than she expected. She had spent so long feeling alone in her struggles, hiding behind her hoodie, her silence, and her insecurities. But maybe Clara was right—she didn't have to face everything alone.

Later that afternoon, Ava found herself standing in front of the classroom door. Inside, students were preparing for their final presentations—the moment when they would share their projects. Her stomach churned, the fear of putting herself out there tightening its grip on her.

She could walk away. No one would blame her if she skipped the presentation. But deep down, Ava knew she had reached the point where she needed to confront the fear head-on. She couldn't keep hiding.

Her mind drifted to Zoe's words: "*You've got more going on than you give yourself credit for. It's time you start seeing that.*"

Ava inhaled deeply, gripping the strap of her backpack. She opened the door and stepped inside, feeling the eyes of her classmates on her. The noise seemed to fade as she found her seat, pulling out her sketchbook, her hands trembling.

When it was Ava's turn, the silence in the room was deafening. She stood at the front of the class, her heart pounding so loudly it drowned out everything else. Her fingers clutched the edge of her sketchbook, her body rigid with fear. "*What if they laugh? What if they don't understand?*"

But there was no turning back now. She slowly flipped open the sketchbook, revealing the artwork she had poured her heart into. It was a self-portrait—raw, unpolished, but real. She had drawn herself not as she wished she could be, but as she was. The imperfections she had always tried to hide were there, front and center.

"*I... I wanted to show something honest*" Ava began, her voice shaky but steadying with each word. "*I've spent so long trying to hide who I am because I was scared people wouldn't like what they saw. But this is me. And I'm learning that being true to myself is what matters.*"

Her words hung in the air, vulnerable but powerful. Ava closed the sketchbook and looked up. For a moment, the room was silent, but it wasn't the harsh, judging silence she had feared. It was something softer, almost understanding.

A soft clap broke the silence, and then another, until the room filled with applause. Ava blinked, surprised by the warmth of the response. It wasn't about whether they loved her art or even understood it—it was about something deeper. She had put herself out there, flaws and all, and the world hadn't crumbled. In fact, it had embraced her.

As Ava sat back down, her heart still racing, Clara leaned over with a smile. "*That was amazing, Ava. You're amazing.*"

Ava didn't know how to respond at first. She felt lighter, freer than she had in a long time. For the first time, she hadn't been performing for others' approval—she had shared a piece of herself, and it had been enough. And maybe, just maybe, she could keep doing that—keep showing the world her true self.

Because she was learning that her true self was more than worthy.

The school bell had rung, signaling the end of the day, as students began to trickle out of the building. Ava lingered near the door for a moment, her heart still fluttering from the presentation. She had done it—stood up there in front of everyone, shared her truth, and survived. Now, as the crowd thinned, she stepped outside, the cool evening air brushing against her skin.

The sun was setting, casting long shadows on the sidewalk as Ava walked home, her sketchbook tucked under her arm. The applause from her presentation still echoed in her mind, a distant reminder of the courage it had taken to stand in front of her classmates and bare a part of her soul. She had expected relief to wash over her, a sense of closure now that the project was behind her.

But instead, there was an unsettling quiet inside her. The thrill of the moment was fading, replaced by lingering doubts. *"What now?"* she wondered. *"Does any of this change how I feel about myself?"*

Ava paused in front of a store window, her reflection caught in the glass. For a moment, she saw the girl she used to be—the one who hid behind baggy clothes and avoided mirrors at all costs. But then she remembered the way she had stood tall in front of her class, the vulnerability in her voice as she shared her art.

Her reflection seemed different now—more familiar, less threatening. She still felt the weight of self-doubt, but it didn't consume her the way it once did. There was something new there—a quiet strength, the beginnings of acceptance.

The next day, Ava found herself standing in the school hallway, her head down as she rummaged through her locker. She wasn't expecting to face the same group of girls who had bullied her so many times before. But there they were—whispers and giggles passing between them as they walked by.

For a brief moment, the old fear returned, the instinct to shrink away, to pull her hoodie closer around herself. *"You're not ready for this"* the voice in her head whispered. *"Nothing's really changed"*.

But then, she remembered the classroom—the way her voice had risen, the way the applause had felt like an acknowledgment of something deeper than her art. And she remembered Zoe's words, *"Confidence doesn't come from trying to be like everyone else. It comes from learning to accept what makes you different."*

Ava straightened her back, refusing to let her fear take over. She didn't need to say anything to the girls; she didn't need to prove herself to them anymore. Instead, she looked them in the eye as they passed, a calm, unwavering expression on her face.

"They don't define me", Ava thought. I know who I am now.

The girls continued walking, their laughter fading into the distance. For the first time, Ava didn't feel small in their presence. She didn't feel the need to hide or defend herself. She felt free.

Later that afternoon, Ava found herself back in the art room. She had returned there after school, drawn by the stillness and the comforting scent of paints and pencils. As she flipped through her sketchbook she thought about how far she had come. Her self-portrait was still imperfect, still raw, but now it felt like a reflection of her journey rather than her flaws.

Just as she was about to pack up, she noticed a younger student lingering by the door. The girl looked hesitant, holding a drawing tightly in her hands. Ava recognized the nervous expression on her face—it was the same fear she had once felt when trying to share her work.

"Hey" Ava called out softly, walking over. *"What's that you've got there?"*

The girl shifted uncomfortably, glancing down at the floor. *"It's just... something I've been working on. But it's not that good."*

Ava smiled, a genuine warmth spreading through her. She knew that feeling too well. *"Can I see?"*

Reluctantly, the girl handed over the drawing. It was rough around the edges, full of scribbled lines and unfinished details, but there was something beautiful in its honesty.

"This is really good." Ava said, handing it back. *"You've got talent."*

The girl looked surprised. *"You really think so?"*

Ava nodded. *"Yeah, I do. Don't be afraid to share it. People will see the heart in your work—just like I did."*

The girl smiled shyly, and Ava felt a swell of pride. She realized, in that moment, that she wasn't just helping someone else—she was also recognizing how far she had come. She had found her voice, her courage, and her self-worth—and now she could share that strength with others.

As she left the art room, the evening light filtering through the windows, Ava felt lighter. The insecurities hadn't vanished completely, and they probably never would. But now she knew that her worth didn't depend on the approval of others. She had the elixir—the understanding that she was valuable and complete, just as she was.

And that was the real reward.

Learning Lessons from "Sketching Strength"

Ava's journey shows you that true confidence isn't about perfection or seeking approval—it's about embracing who you are, flaws and all. The path to self-acceptance begins when you stop comparing yourself to others and start appreciating your unique qualities. Just like Ava discovered through her art, your imperfections are part of what makes you real, relatable, and beautifully human.

Comparison can be a heavy burden, pulling you away from your own worth. Ava learned that the people who matter most aren't the ones judging her from a distance—they're the ones who see her heart, her talent, and her strength. When you shift your focus from others' opinions to your own journey, you begin to see the beauty in what you offer to the world.

Courage doesn't mean being unafraid—it means stepping forward even when you're scared. By sharing her self-portrait, Ava found the strength to stand in her truth, not for approval but for herself. In doing so, she inspired others and created space for connection and understanding.

Let Ava's story remind you: you are enough as you are. Share your voice, your talents, and your authentic self with the world—because your story is worth telling, and it will resonate more deeply than you imagine.

Story 4 - The Art of Being True

The day was like any other at Westbrook High, but for Emma, each morning felt like stepping onto a battlefield. Walking down the hall, she glanced at the clusters of girls who seemed to have it all together—flawless makeup, designer clothes, and a confidence she could only dream of. As she approached her locker, she overheard whispers and giggles. Emma's fingers tightened around the straps of her backpack, and her eyes shifted to her reflection in the locker door's dull metal. Was she invisible? Or worse, did they see her and not care?

"Why do I never fit in?" she thought, her heart sinking. *"If I could just change something—anything—maybe they'd notice me. Maybe I wouldn't feel so out of place."*

She tugged at the sleeves of her worn-out hoodie, pulling it tighter around her like a shield. The weight of self-doubt hung over her, as familiar as the bell that rang overhead, marking the start of yet another day where she felt like a spectator to her own life.

Emma shuffled into her classroom, taking her usual seat near the back. The chatter of her classmates filled the room, but she kept her gaze down, focusing on the notebook in front of her. She scribbled aimlessly, trying to blend into the background, when a voice cut through the noise, drawing her attention.

Jade, one of the popular girls, turned to Emma with a half-smile, her eyes scanning Emma's outfit. *"You know, Emma, you'd look so cute if you just... tried a little harder. Maybe wear something that shows off your figure."* She paused, as if considering her next words carefully. *"We're all going to the mall this weekend. You should come. We could help you find something to bring out your best."*

For a second, Emma's heart skipped. Was this it? Was this her chance to finally belong—to stop feeling like an outsider looking in? She could almost picture it: laughing with Jade and her friends, walking through the halls with confidence. All she had to do was say yes, and maybe, just maybe, she wouldn't feel so alone anymore.

But as the vision played out in her mind, a knot of discomfort twisted in her stomach. Something didn't feel right. Was this really what she wanted? Was this really her?

Later that afternoon, Emma found herself standing in front of her mirror at home, staring at her reflection. The invitation replayed in her mind, but with each passing moment, the excitement she had felt earlier began to fade. The clothes she usually wore—a mix of quirky t-shirts and jeans—felt like an extension of who she was, even if they didn't fit the popular group's idea of trendy.

Her fingers traced the outline of her hoodie again, her safest armor against the world's judgment.

"If I go with them, I'll have to change everything about myself. I'm not sure I can do that." The thought settled heavily, pulling her back into her cocoon of self-doubt. *"But if I don't go, what if I never get a chance to fit in?"*

That evening, Aunt Karen dropped by for dinner. She had always been someone Emma could talk to, someone who seemed to understand the struggles of teenage life without judgment. As they sat in the living room afterward, Karen noticed the far-off look in Emma's eyes.

"Something on your mind, sweetie?"

Emma hesitated for a moment but then spilled everything—the invitation, the expectations, the pressure to be someone she wasn't.

Karen listened patiently, her eyes soft and understanding. *"You know, when I was your age, I tried to fit in with the 'cool' crowd too'"* she began, a knowing smile playing at her lips. *"It didn't take long for me to realize that no matter how hard I tried, I was never going to be them. I spent so much energy trying to change myself that I forgot the parts of me that made me happy, the parts that made me... well, me."*

Emma's eyes widened, surprised at how much Karen's story mirrored her own. *"But what did you do?"* she asked.

"I stopped pretending." Karen said simply. *"And I realized that the right people—the ones who truly matter—will like you for who you are, not who you try to be."*

Karen's words lingered with Emma long after their conversation ended. The next day, as she stood at her locker, she saw Jade and the others in the distance, laughing, carefree. Emma felt a familiar pang of longing, but this time, something inside her had shifted.

She could still feel the pull to fit in with them, but she also felt the weight of Karen's advice: being true to herself would lead her down a better path. Taking a deep breath, she made a decision. She would go to the mall with Jade and her friends, but she wouldn't become someone else just to fit in.

Her heart raced as she walked up to the group. *"Hey, about this weekend..."* she began, her voice soft but steady. *"I'll come. But I don't want to change everything about myself. I like who I am."*

The look on Jade's face was a mix of surprise and confusion, but Emma didn't flinch. For the first time, she felt the stirrings of strength—like she had taken a step closer to discovering who she really was.

The weekend arrived faster than she expected. Emma found herself walking toward the mall, her mind racing with a mix of anticipation and dread. She had promised herself she wouldn't change, but now, with every step, the pressure to conform felt heavier. She could feel the weight of Jade's expectations looming.

Emma stood outside the clothing store, a pit forming in her stomach. She had agreed to go shopping with Jade and the popular girls, hoping to blend in and finally feel like she belonged. But now, under the bright lights and surrounded by racks of clothes she would never choose for herself, the reality of the situation hit her hard.

Jade pulled a dress from the rack, holding it up to Emma's frame. "*This will look so cute on you.*" she said, a smile tugging at her lips. "*Try it on.*"

Emma took the dress reluctantly, staring at the delicate fabric. It was the kind of outfit she knew would make her feel uncomfortable—too tight, too revealing, too not her. But Jade's expectant gaze left her feeling trapped. Did she really want this? To wear something that didn't reflect who she was just to gain their approval?

As Emma disappeared into the fitting room, she caught sight of herself in the mirror. The reflection staring back at her looked more uncertain than ever. Who was she becoming? She felt torn—part of her wanted to belong, but another part screamed that this wasn't the way.

"*Why am I doing this? To fit in? But at what cost?*" The thought lingered as she tried on the dress, feeling the fabric cling to her body in all the wrong ways. She stepped out, forcing a smile as the girls gasped in admiration, but inside, she felt hollow.

When Jade insisted she buy the dress, Emma hesitated, but under the weight of their expectations, she found herself nodding. She handed over the money, the fabric folded into a shopping bag—along with a piece of herself.

The rest of the shopping trip passed in a blur. Emma nodded along as the others chatted about trends and fashion, but her mind was elsewhere. The more she tried to blend in, the more disconnected she felt from herself. By the time she got home, the weight of the day hung over her like a cloud.

That night, Emma sat at her desk, her sketchbook untouched. She used to draw when she was feeling overwhelmed, letting her creativity flow to make sense of her thoughts. But lately, she hadn't picked up her pencil at all. It was as if trying to fit into the popular group had drained her of everything that made her feel like herself.

Her phone buzzed. A message from Jade: *"Can't wait to see you at school tomorrow in that dress!"*

Emma's heart sank. The thought of walking into school wearing something that felt so wrong left her feeling physically sick. She stared at her phone screen, her fingers hovering over the keyboard.

"Do I really want this?" she wondered. *"What am I trying to prove, and to whom?"*

The next day, Emma stood in front of the mirror in her bedroom, dressed in the new outfit. Her reflection was a stranger—someone she barely recognized. The dress clung too tightly, the style far removed from anything she would have chosen for herself. But there she was, about to walk out the door, feeling like an imposter in her own skin.

She stepped into school, every step feeling heavier than the last. The popular girls waved her over, their eyes gleaming with approval, but Emma's discomfort only grew. She caught glimpses of herself in the glass windows as she passed by, and with every glance, a pit of dread formed deeper in her chest.

By lunchtime, the pressure became unbearable. She excused herself from the group and found a quiet spot outside, away from the crowd. Emma slumped against the wall, her chest tightening as tears threatened to spill. This wasn't who she was. She had tried so hard to be someone else, but in doing so, she had lost herself.

Her mind raced, replaying Karen's words from their conversation a few nights ago: *"The right people will like you for who you are, not who you pretend to be."*

In that moment, the realization hit her—she didn't need to fit into someone else's mold to be valued. The real Emma, the girl who wore quirky clothes and sketched in her free time, was worthy just as she was. She always had been.

Emma straightened, a sense of clarity washing over her. She pulled her phone from her pocket and typed a message to Jade: *"I can't do this anymore. This isn't me."* Her heart pounded as she hit send, but for the first time in weeks, she felt lighter.

Back at home, Emma grabbed her sketchbook, flipping to a blank page. She began to draw, the lines flowing from her pencil effortlessly, as if she were rediscovering a part of herself she had hidden away. She smiled to herself, her mind clear. This was who she was—a creative, kind, unique person, and that was everything she needed to be.

As she worked on her art, she felt the layers of insecurity and doubt peel away. Emma didn't need to be popular to be happy. What mattered was that she could finally look at herself in the mirror and recognize the person staring back.

It had been a few days since Emma sent the message to Jade and made the decision to embrace her true self. Now, as she walked down the hallway at school, the same halls that used to feel like a battlefield, things felt different. Lighter. She wasn't hiding anymore. Instead of avoiding eye contact or shrinking into herself, she held her head a little higher, her steps a little more sure. But the road back to herself wasn't without its challenges.

As Emma passed by the group of popular girls, she braced herself for their reaction. Jade glanced her way, but this time, there was no approving smile, no friendly wave. Instead, there was only indifference—a cool, dismissive glance that cut through Emma more than she had expected. For a moment, doubt flickered in her mind. Had she made the right choice?

"Maybe I should have just kept trying to fit in," Emma thought, her stomach twisting as she quickened her pace. But as soon as the thought entered her mind, she shook it off. *No.* She knew deep down that she

had finally chosen the right path—her path. The road back wasn't about winning anyone's approval; it was about finding peace with who she was.

Later that afternoon, Emma sat in the school's art room, sketchbook in hand, lost in the calming rhythm of pencil against paper. This was her safe space, the place where she could breathe freely and express herself without judgment. As she shaded in the final details of her drawing—a reflection of herself standing confidently under an open sky—she felt a sense of renewal. The quiet murmur of the art room surrounded her, grounding her in the present moment.

A knock on the door interrupted her thoughts. Karen stepped in, a warm smile on her face. "*How's my favorite artist doing?*" she asked, leaning against the doorway.

Emma smiled, looking down at her drawing. "*Better. I think I'm finally figuring things out.*"

Karen walked over, glancing at the sketchbook. "*You know*" she said, her voice gentle, "*the fact that you were brave enough to stand up for who you are—it's something a lot of people never figure out. Not until much later.*"

Emma looked at her mentor, feeling a swell of pride in her chest. "*It wasn't easy*", she admitted, her voice softer. "*There are still moments where I wonder if I made the right choice... but I don't want to go back to pretending. I'm tired of being someone I'm not.*"

Karen nodded, placing a reassuring hand on her shoulder. "*It takes time. But you're already so much stronger than you realize, Emma.*"

As Karen left, Emma stared down at the sketch again. Her hand hovered over the page, adding a final touch to the sky—an arc of light cutting through the clouds. It was a symbol of her own resurrection, a reminder that she had risen above the expectations of others and found strength in her individuality.

The day of the school's "Self-Expression Day" came faster than Emma anticipated. It wasn't a talent show or a competition—just an opportunity for students to showcase something that mattered to them, something that reflected who they truly were. It was exactly the kind of moment Emma needed.

This wasn't about proving herself to others; it was about embracing who she was. Her art had always been a part of her, a private way of processing the world, and now she was ready to share it in a way she never had before.

As the students wandered through the gym-turned-gallery, Emma stood by her artwork—her sketch of the confident figure standing under an open sky. The drawing captured her journey: the struggle of self-doubt, the weight of expectations, and finally, the freedom that came from embracing her uniqueness.

A small crowd gathered near her piece, and Emma's heart fluttered as she caught snippets of admiration from her classmates. But this time, the nervousness wasn't overpowering—it was mixed with something else: a quiet, steady confidence.

One student approached her. *"This drawing is amazing."* she said. *"It's like I can feel what you're saying through the lines."*

Emma smiled, her fingers gently tracing the edges of her sketchbook. *"It's how I express myself"* she said, feeling a sense of calm as the words left her lips. *"I used to think I had to be like everyone else to fit in. But I've learned that it's okay to just be me. That's what this is about."*

As more students passed by, admiring her work, Emma stood tall, no longer trying to fade into the background. The day wasn't about applause or external validation; it was about recognizing her own worth.

When the event ended, Emma walked out of the gym, her heart light. The weight of trying to conform had been lifted, replaced with the certainty that she didn't need to fit anyone else's mold. She had found her voice, her confidence, and a renewed sense of self-worth. The elixir she gained was the quiet understanding that she was enough, just as she was—her art, her voice, her individuality.

This time, the approval of others wasn't what mattered most. Emma had learned to value herself.

Learning Lessons from "The Art of Being True"

Emma's journey reminds you that real strength comes from embracing who you are, not from conforming to others' expectations. Trying to fit into someone else's mold can leave you feeling lost and disconnected, but the truth is, you don't need to change yourself to find acceptance or happiness. Your individuality—your quirks, passions, and unique traits—is what makes you special.

Sometimes, the pressure to belong can feel overwhelming, and it's tempting to trade your authenticity for approval. But as Emma discovered, the cost of pretending to be someone you're not is far greater than the temporary comfort of fitting in. By choosing to honor her true self, Emma found a deeper sense of belonging—not with the popular crowd, but within herself.

This story shows you that self-expression is a powerful tool for finding clarity and confidence. Whether through art, writing, or simply being yourself, sharing your authentic voice can connect you to others in meaningful ways. The right people will see your worth without you needing to change a thing.

Let Emma's experience encourage you to stand tall in your individuality and trust in your unique gifts. The journey to self-acceptance isn't always easy, but it's worth it. Each step you take toward being true to yourself helps you discover your inner strength and value.

Remember, you don't need to seek approval from others to feel whole. Like Emma, you can find freedom in letting go of comparisons and embracing what makes you, you. Your authenticity is your greatest strength, and the more you honor it, the more you'll inspire others to do the same.

Story 5 - This is me

The late afternoon sun filtered through the blinds, casting soft shadows on Maya's bedroom walls. She sat at her desk, sketching absentmindedly in a notebook that was usually reserved for school assignments. The paper was littered with doodles of random shapes, none of them making much sense. Maya's eyes kept drifting toward the open closet door, where a pile of clothes lay crumpled on the floor. Her favorite pair of jeans, the ones that always used to fit just right, now felt tight and uncomfortable around her waist.

She stared at the clothes with frustration. *"Why do they all look so good in their outfits while I feel like I'm hiding?"* she thought. Her friends had started showing off new dresses and fitted tops, laughing about weekend plans, while Maya avoided looking in the mirror. It seemed like every glance at her reflection was a reminder of how much her body was changing—and not in a way she liked. Her skin wasn't as smooth anymore, and her once-favorite shirts now clung awkwardly in all the wrong places.

A gentle knock at the door broke her from her thoughts. Her mom's voice floated in, "Maya, dinner's ready."

Maya sighed, dropping her pencil. *"Why am I the only one who feels so out of place?"* she wondered, standing up slowly and eyeing the mirror beside her desk. She caught a glimpse of her reflection and quickly looked away. Her body didn't feel like her own anymore—too many changes happening all at once, and she wasn't sure how to handle any of them.

Dinner that night was the same as always—Mom asking about her day, her little brother chattering away, and Maya barely able to pay attention. She could feel her clothes clinging to her uncomfortably. It was then that her mom looked over at her with a thoughtful smile. *"Maya, we're going shopping for new clothes this weekend. How about we find you something that makes you feel comfortable and confident?"*

Maya's heart sank. Shopping meant trying things on, standing in front of mirrors under those harsh dressing room lights, and facing the body she was trying so hard to avoid. Her mom meant well, but the thought of putting herself out there like that terrified her.

Later that evening, Maya lay in bed, staring up at the ceiling. *"I don't want to go shopping,"* she thought. *"What's the point? Nothing fits right anymore. Everything feels wrong."* She turned over, pulling her blanket tight around her, wishing she could just disappear. The idea of stepping into a store, of having to confront the changes in her body, filled her with dread.

"What if I never like how I look again? What if I keep growing and I never feel like myself?" The fear clung to her, heavy and suffocating. She couldn't imagine feeling good in her body again, let alone trying on new clothes to mask how out of place she felt.

The next day, while helping her mom clear the dishes after breakfast, her older cousin Emma dropped by unexpectedly. Emma was in college now, and Maya always admired her effortless confidence. As they sat down for a chat, Emma seemed to sense something was off. *"Hey, what's on your mind, Maya?"*

Maya hesitated, then blurted out, "*I hate how I look. My body feels so weird, and it's like... nothing fits. It's embarrassing.*"

Emma smiled softly. "*You know, I felt the same way when I was your age. I didn't recognize myself in the mirror for a long time. I remember being angry at my body for changing, like it was doing something wrong.*" Maya's eyes widened—she had no idea Emma went through this too. "*But your body isn't the enemy, Maya.*" Emma continued. "*It's growing and changing because that's what it's supposed to do. It's not about trying to control it; it's about learning to accept and respect it.*"

Emma reached for her wrist, revealing a delicate bracelet with a small charm. "*My mom gave this to me when I was going through what you are now.*" she said, her voice soft but reassuring. "It reminded me that no matter what changes were happening, I was growing into who I was meant to be. It's a reminder to trust the process, even when it feels uncomfortable."

She hesitated for a moment, then unhooked the bracelet and gently placed it in Maya's hand. "*Here*" Emma said, her eyes warm with understanding. "*Take it. You're becoming more of who you're meant to be every day. It might not feel that way now, but trust me—you'll see it soon enough.*"

Maya took the bracelet, feeling its weight in her hand. It wasn't just a bracelet—it was a symbol of Emma's understanding, a reminder that this journey wasn't one she had to face alone.

On Saturday, Maya and her mom went to the local mall to pick out some new clothes. The store's bright lights and rows of neatly hung outfits made Maya feel a bit overwhelmed, but she followed her mom to the dressing room area. Now, standing in front of the dressing room mirror, her mom waited patiently outside. The familiar anxiety bubbled up as she looked at the pile of clothes she was supposed to try on. But then she glanced down at the bracelet on her wrist, Emma's words echoing in her mind: "*It's not about controlling it; it's about accepting it.*"

Taking a deep breath, Maya reached for the first outfit. It wasn't about perfection; it was about trying. As she slipped the clothes on, she glanced at herself in the mirror—noticing the small changes, the things she hadn't accepted yet—but this time, she didn't immediately turn away. The reflection wasn't perfect, but it was real.

She stepped out of the dressing room, where her mom was waiting. *"How do you feel?"* her mom asked, her eyes kind and encouraging.

Maya smiled, a small but genuine smile. *"It's... okay"* she replied. For the first time, she wasn't running from herself. She had crossed a threshold—one that wouldn't erase all her doubts, but one that showed her she didn't have to fight her body anymore. The real journey was just beginning.

The Monday morning after the shopping trip, Maya walked into school feeling a mixture of relief and unease. The new clothes from the weekend fit comfortably, but when she saw herself in the mirror that morning, she still didn't quite recognize the girl staring back at her. Returning to her usual routine felt like stepping back into a battlefield. As she made her way through the bustling hallways, Maya couldn't help but notice her classmates—some still looked the same as always, while others seemed to be transforming overnight, their bodies growing into curves, their skin glowing. She felt left behind.

At lunch, her closest friend Chloe sat across from her in the noisy cafeteria. Chloe had always been athletic and fit, seemingly immune to the awkwardness Maya felt trapped in. *"I've started running again"* Chloe said, pushing her salad around her plate. *"You should join me! It might help, you know, get you in shape."*

Maya's stomach twisted. *"In shape?"* The words echoed in her mind, biting sharper than Chloe intended. Was Chloe hinting that she didn't look right—that she needed to change even more? The suggestion felt like an unspoken judgment, and Maya's thoughts spiraled. Maybe she *wasn't* enough as she was. Maybe she really did need to "fix" herself.

Chloe's words lingered in Maya's mind long after lunch. *"Maybe she's right. Maybe running will help me feel better"*. But even as she considered it, a sense of frustration bubbled up. *"Why does it feel like I have to keep changing? Why can't I just be okay with who I am?"*

Maya's confidence faltered again, and the self-doubt she had fought so hard to push away started creeping back in.

After school, Maya retreated to the solitude of her room, feeling more disconnected from her body than ever. She stood in front of the mirror, tugging at the fabric of her new shirt. The clothes fit, but they still didn't feel like *her*. It was as if her body had a mind of its own, and she was just a passenger in it, trying to keep up.

Emma's bracelet, the one she'd given her for reassurance, caught the light as it sat on her wrist. It had been a comfort—until now. In the soft evening glow, Maya slid it off, setting it gently on her dresser. *"I'm not sure I can do this,"* she whispered. The reflection staring back at her looked unsure, trapped between wanting to change and wanting to hold on to who she used to be.

Just as Maya's thoughts drifted to Emma, her phone buzzed unexpectedly. She glanced down at the screen—it was a message from Emma: "Remember, your body is your journey. No one else's."

The timing felt almost eerie, like Emma somehow knew what she was thinking. It was a small reminder, but it hit deeply. Emma's words hung in the air, soft yet powerful.

Maya sank onto her bed, thinking. She knew Emma was right, but that didn't stop the overwhelming feelings that twisted her thoughts. "I want to accept myself, but how do I stop feeling like I'm falling short?"

The next day at school, Maya was faced with a new challenge—a pool party invite from her friend group. It should've been fun, but the idea of wearing a swimsuit in front of everyone felt like a nightmare. Standing in front of her locker, Maya overheard a group of girls laughing nearby. *"I'm going to wear the new bikini I got this weekend."* one of them boasted. *"I've been hitting the gym to make sure I look perfect."*

Maya froze. The words stung. She could feel the same old panic rise in her chest. Could she really show up at the party? What if people saw her in a swimsuit and judged her? What if they whispered, just like those girls?

That night, Maya sat by her window, staring at the sky. The moon hung low, casting soft shadows across her room. *"I can't do it,"* she thought, *"I don't belong at that party. Not like this."*

But something inside her stirred, a small voice reminding her that she had already taken the first step. *"You've started this journey. Why turn back now?"* the voice whispered.

Maya's thoughts shifted. *"Maybe I'm not perfect, but do I really want to spend my life hiding? Or pretending to be something I'm not?"* The reflection in her window wasn't as sharp as the one in her mirror, but for the first time in a long while, Maya didn't mind it. *"Maybe I can try."*

The day of the pool party arrived, and as Maya stood in front of her mirror one last time, she took a deep breath. She wasn't completely confident, but she wasn't running either. She slipped on a one-piece swimsuit that made her feel comfortable, not because it hid her, but because it felt like *her.* It was the first real decision she had made about her body that didn't come from fear or embarrassment—it came from a place of self-respect.

When she arrived at the party, she could feel eyes on her, but this time, she didn't shy away. Chloe waved her over, her smile warm and genuine. *"You look great, Maya"* she said, and Maya could feel that it wasn't just about appearances—it was about how she carried herself.

As Maya joined in the fun, splashing around with her friends, she realized that she had faced one of her biggest fears. She wasn't hiding anymore, and it felt like a victory, no matter how small. The world hadn't ended because she wasn't perfect. She had shown up, just as she was, and that was enough.

"Maybe this is what Emma meant," Maya thought as the afternoon sunset at the party. *"It's not about changing everything. It's about showing up, about giving myself the chance to be okay with who I am, step by step."*

A week had passed since the pool party, and Maya found herself standing in front of her bedroom mirror once again. The familiar tug of self-doubt hadn't disappeared, and the changes in her body hadn't either. But something felt different—not so much in her reflection, but in how she viewed herself.

The pool party had been a turning point—a moment when she had chosen not to hide but to embrace where she was. That small decision had started to shift things inside her. The mirror, which once felt like an enemy, now felt more like a companion on her journey—reflecting a girl still evolving, still learning.

Maya gathered her sketchbook, pausing to take one last glance in the mirror. *"I'm not completely there yet, but maybe that's okay"* she thought, a small smile tugging at her lips. Her conversation with Emma echoed in her mind, reminding her that growth wasn't about achieving perfection, but about embracing the messiness of change.

"You're evolving, Maya. And that's what matters" she remembered Emma telling her. And for the first time, Maya felt like she was beginning to believe it.

The next day at school, Maya felt the usual nervous energy bubbling beneath the surface, but she also felt stronger. Walking through the halls, she noticed the stares from some classmates but didn't shrink from them this time. She could feel their eyes on her, comparing her new curves to the girls who hadn't yet changed—or the ones who already had—but Maya didn't look away. Instead, she held her head high.

Chloe, her closest friend, jogged up beside her. *"You good for the presentation later?"* Chloe asked, noticing Maya's calmness.

"Yeah, actually, I am." Ava replied, surprised at the confidence in her own voice.

They were preparing for a class project where everyone had to present something personal, something meaningful. For Maya, the choice was clear. She had chosen to present a collection of her sketches—each one a reflection of her body at different stages, documenting the very changes that had once caused her so much anxiety.

As she stood at the front of the classroom, Maya hesitated for just a moment. The familiar self-consciousness washed over her, but this time, something else pushed forward—the strength to be seen as she truly was.

"I've spent a lot of time being embarrassed by my body." Maya began, her voice clear but soft. *"I kept comparing myself to everyone else, wondering why I wasn't changing like them—or why I was changing too fast."* She flipped open her sketchbook, revealing pages of detailed, raw sketches from when her body started shifting to the present.

"But I'm learning that these changes aren't something to hide from. They're just part of growing up." she continued, her gaze meeting her classmates. *"We all go through them differently, and that's okay. This is my journey, and I'm finally starting to appreciate it."*

The room was silent as Maya let her words sink in. For the first time in a long while, she didn't feel small or out of place. She felt proud.

After school, Maya walked home, the late afternoon sun warming her face. There was a lightness in her step, as if the weight she'd been carrying had finally lifted. Her body hadn't changed overnight—her curves, the fluctuations in her weight, the occasional breakout—they were still there. But now, she didn't feel the same shame she used to. She had something much more powerful: self-acceptance.

As she reached her front porch, Maya paused. She pulled out her sketchbook again, flipping to a blank page. Her fingers traced over the empty space as she thought about everything she had been through. This was her story, and she was in control of how it unfolded.

At that moment, Maya realized she had found her elixir—not in the form of a perfect body or flawless skin, but in the knowledge that her body was just one part of her. It didn't define her worth. She was strong, creative, and evolving. She had her insecurities, yes, but she also had something greater: resilience.

"This is me." Maya thought as she began to draw again, lines flowing effortlessly across the page. *"And I'm finally okay with that."*

Learning Lessons from "This is Me"

Your body is a story of growth, change, and resilience. Maya's journey shows that it's okay to feel uncertain or uncomfortable as you navigate changes in your appearance or how you see yourself. What matters is finding the courage to embrace the process and understand that your worth goes far beyond how you look.

Comparing yourself to others—whether it's friends, classmates, or what you see online—can make you feel like you're falling short. But just like Maya realized, everyone's journey is different, and there's no one "right" way to grow or change. What makes you unique is what makes you strong.

Sometimes, the first step to self-acceptance is choosing to face the things that scare you. Whether it's trying something new, wearing what makes you feel comfortable, or simply standing tall in your own skin, those small decisions can build a foundation of confidence.

It's also important to lean on those who care about you, like Maya did with Emma. Honest conversations with trusted friends or family can remind you that you don't have to go through this alone.

Finally, remember that self-acceptance doesn't happen overnight. It's a process, one step at a time. Each day you show up for yourself, you grow closer to understanding that you are more than enough, just as you are.

Story 6 - True to Me

The morning sunlight spilled through the wide café windows, casting a warm glow on the small tables and chairs, each lovingly arranged by Lena's mom before dawn. Lena, fourteen and thoughtful, swept crumbs from the counter as she prepared for another day at her family's seaside café. She loved the familiar rhythm here—the soft whir of the coffee grinder, the smell of fresh bread in the oven, and the occasional hum of tourists mingling with locals. Yet today, her chest felt tight, a sense of unease pressing down like a storm cloud on a clear day.

"Maybe skip the muffin today, sweetheart" her mother's voice came from behind, casual but edged with a tone Lena knew too well. *"Let's focus on something lighter."*

Lena's hand froze as she reached for a freshly baked blueberry muffin. She managed a nod, swallowing the lump in her throat. Her mom and Sophie, her older sister, always seemed to have a gentle reminder about what she should or shouldn't eat. The words were always framed as "for her health," but each one chipped away a little at her self-worth. She knew her family meant well, but why did her love for food always feel like something to hide?

Later that afternoon, Lena took her usual spot by the window to people-watch during the café's slow hours. She noticed her mother and Sophie exchanging glances as they discussed a "health cleanse" they were planning. Her mother called out to her, "*Maybe you'd like to join us, Lena? We could all support each other and start some healthy habits as a family.*"

Lena's heart sank. The message was clear: she wasn't exactly what they hoped she'd be. Part of her longed to join them, to fit in with the healthy, slim image they seemed to celebrate, but the thought felt heavy, like giving up a part of herself. She loved food and the joy it brought to her, and the idea of restricting herself felt wrong. But a small voice inside wondered if she should try—if maybe changing herself would ease the tension in her family.

She hesitated. "*I... I'll think about it*" Lena replied softly, her voice barely audible. Her mom smiled, clearly encouraged, but Lena could feel her stomach churn. This was her family, and she wanted their approval, yet their expectations left her feeling small and out of place.

That evening, she sat in her room, staring into her mirror. "*Why can't I just be okay as I am?*" she whispered to herself, feeling both frustrated and hurt. The familiar reflection stared back, but all she could see were the flaws that her family seemed to notice too.

The next day, as Lena cleaned up after the lunch rush, Rosa entered the café—a frequent regular with an easy laugh and a colorful scarf wrapped around her hair. Rosa had a way of seeing things others didn't, and today, she caught Lena's downcast eyes as she leaned against the counter.

"*Hey, Lena, why the long face?*" Rosa asked, her voice warm and inviting.

Lena shrugged, hesitating, but there was something about Rosa's gentle gaze that invited honesty. "*It's just... sometimes, I feel like I'm not what my family wants me to be. They're always talking about health and what I should eat, but it makes me feel like I'm... wrong.*"

Rosa's face softened. She reached into her bag and pulled out a small, worn sketchbook. "*When I was your age, I felt the same way. I was so focused on what other people thought of me that I forgot to get to know myself.*" She handed the sketchbook to Lena. "*Maybe this can be your space. Draw, write, scribble—whatever you need. It's a way of listening to yourself and learning that your own voice matters just as much as anyone else's.*"

Lena took the sketchbook, feeling a glimmer of something new—a sense that her thoughts, her identity, could have a safe place, even if it was only on paper. "*Thanks, Rosa*" she said quietly, feeling both grateful and a little hopeful.

That night, Lena sat on her bed, the sketchbook open on her lap. She picked up her pencil, uncertain at first. She started with small lines, drawing shapes that mirrored the confusion she felt inside. Her family's voices echoed in her mind, but here, on the page, she let her thoughts flow without judgment.

After a few moments, she began to sketch an image—a girl standing on a cliff by the sea, the wind blowing her hair. The girl looked strong, unbothered by the waves crashing below her. Lena paused, realizing that this figure, standing confidently, was what she wanted to be: someone who wasn't swayed by others' expectations.

As she set her pencil down, Lena felt a quiet resolve form inside her. Maybe she wasn't ready to confront her family directly, but she would start by honoring herself, just as Rosa had suggested. This was her first step—a small but powerful act of claiming her voice.

As summer settled in, the café buzzed with customers seeking a cool drink or a shady spot. Lena worked behind the counter, filling orders, but her thoughts drifted to the comments her mother had made earlier about her outfit. "*A looser fit would be better, Lena. We're representing our family here.*" her mother had said, her tone kind but unmistakably critical. Each remark felt like a pebble, small but slowly forming a weight she carried with her.

Sophie breezed by, laughing with a group of friends who'd dropped by. She threw Lena a casual glance and murmured, *"Mom's right, you know. It's just about presenting your best self."* Lena wanted to argue, but something in Sophie's tone made her falter. Instead, she plastered on a smile, though her stomach churned with unease.

Later that afternoon, Rosa came into the café and waved to Lena, who was clearing tables by the window. Seeing her, Lena felt a swell of relief. Rosa had become an ally, someone who saw beyond surface appearances.

"You look distracted, Lena" Rosa observed gently, sitting down at one of the tables as Lena continued to clear the others.

Lena hesitated before responding, unsure of how to put her feelings into words. Finally, she said, *"It's just... everyone seems to have an opinion on who I should be, how I should look. Sometimes I don't even recognize myself when I look in the mirror."*

Rosa's expression softened. *"That's hard. But remember, Lena—only you can decide what feels right for you. The mirror only shows one part of you; there's so much more beneath the surface."*

Lena nodded, feeling a glimmer of reassurance. It was as though Rosa's words granted her permission to hold onto herself, even in the face of others' expectations.

A few days later, one quiet evening, Lena sat on her bed with Rosa's sketchbook open on her lap. She began to scribble her feelings in raw, jagged lines across the page, eventually sketching a figure standing on a cliff, its features blurred, uncertain. It was an image of herself, she realized—someone caught between who she wanted to be and who others expected her to become.

"Why do I care so much?" she thought. *"Why can't I just let it go?"*

But she knew the answer. They were her family. She loved them, and their approval mattered. Yet the constant criticism, even when veiled as "helpful advice" left her feeling torn. She wanted to meet their expectations, but it came at the cost of her peace of mind. She couldn't keep twisting herself into something she wasn't.

The next day, Lena's mom suggested a family outing, an evening walk on the beach with her parents and Sophie. They walked in companionable silence for a while, the sound of waves crashing softly against the shore. Lena felt the weight of unspoken words pressing on her, yet unsure if she had the courage to speak up.

Eventually, her mother broke the silence. *"You know, Lena, if you wanted, we could start a new exercise plan together. Just to keep each other accountable"* her mom suggested, her tone light but laced with the familiar edge Lena had come to dread.

Lena's breath caught, and a wave of frustration surged within her. She stopped walking, the sand cool under her feet as she turned to her mother. *"Mom... can we just walk without talking about my body or my diet? It makes me feel like... like I'm not good enough the way I am."*

Her mom looked taken aback, clearly not expecting such a reaction. *"Lena, that's not what I meant at all. I just want you to be happy and healthy."*

"I know you mean well" Lena replied, trying to steady her voice. "But it doesn't feel like that to me. It just feels... like pressure."

A quiet understanding passed between them, and her mother nodded slowly, a mixture of surprise and consideration in her expression. For the first time, Lena felt like she had allowed herself to set a boundary, to voice her discomfort instead of internalizing it.

That evening, Lena returned to her room and opened her sketchbook, feeling lighter. She sketched a figure again, but this time, it was standing on solid ground, looking out toward the horizon with a sense of calm. The lines were bolder, more defined—no longer blurred and uncertain.

As she looked at her drawing, a sense of empowerment washed over her. Speaking up hadn't been easy, but it had been worth it. She felt closer to herself, more connected to her thoughts and feelings than she had in a long time.

Before going to bed, she whispered to herself, "*I don't have to change for anyone. I can just be... me.*" And for the first time, that felt truly right.

On the next day, Sophie, her older sister, was arranging baked goods at the counter. "*Hey, Lena!*" she said, her tone casual but holding an undercurrent of curiosity. "*I was thinking, maybe we could try out a few healthy recipes together. It might be fun, you know?*"

Lena paused, her fingers instinctively tightening around her sketchbook. In the past, she might have brushed off the suggestion or gone along with it to avoid tension. But today, Rosa's words echoed in her mind: "*Healthy boundaries are about finding what feels right for you, not just others.*"

She took a breath and replied, "*Thanks, Sophie. I know you mean well. But I'm actually okay with the things I enjoy already. Maybe I can share a recipe I love sometime?*"

Sophie looked slightly taken aback but nodded. "*Sure, Lena. I'd like that.*" she replied, a mix of understanding and newfound respect in her eyes.

That evening, Lena's family gathered around the table for dinner, the usual spread of homemade dishes in front of them. Her mother began, casually mentioning portion sizes and "*balance*" as she had so often before. Normally, Lena would stay silent, bracing herself against the quiet discomfort these conversations caused. But tonight was different.

Lena looked around the table, and as she saw her mother and Sophie talking, she realized that she wanted a family dynamic rooted in acceptance—not pressure. With her heart pounding, she cleared her throat. "*Mom, Sophie,*" she began, her voice softer than she intended but growing stronger as she continued, "*I really want to be healthy, but I also want to feel good about myself. When there are so many comments about my choices, it's hard for me to feel that way.*"

Her mother and Sophie looked at her, and surprise was evident on their faces. Her mother opened her mouth to respond, but Lena gently continued, "*I know you care and want the best for me, and I appreciate that. I just need to figure out what healthy means for me.*"

A moment of silence followed, and then her mother nodded slowly. "*Thank you for sharing that, Lena. I hadn't realized how it was affecting you.*" There was a new softness in her mother's eyes, a glimmer of understanding Lena had longed for.

Sophie added, "*I think it's brave of you to speak up, Lena. It's not easy.*"

Lena nodded, feeling a rush of relief. She hadn't expected them to change overnight, but voicing her feelings and setting her boundaries felt like a significant victory.

The next morning, Lena walked down to the beach, sketchbook in hand. She found her favorite spot, overlooking the waves, and began drawing—a girl standing tall, with an open stance, facing the ocean's vastness. Each line she sketched reflected her own journey from doubt and confusion to clarity and self-respect.

The scene represented her growth: her journey to embrace who she was without the need for external approval. She had found her own definition of health and beauty—one that included kindness, self-care, and personal joy.

As she closed her sketchbook and looked out over the ocean, a calm sense of fulfillment washed over her. She knew she'd return to the café and her family with the courage to remain true to herself, even as she navigated their well-intentioned but sometimes challenging expectations.

For the first time, Lena felt that her voice mattered. She had gained something far more precious than the validation of others—she had gained an unwavering sense of self. And as she stood there, waves crashing softly against the shore, she knew she was ready to embrace each new day with confidence and an open heart.

Learning Lessons from True to Me

Lena's journey reminds you that your worth is not tied to others' expectations or opinions. It's easy to internalize well-meaning comments, especially from family or loved ones, but your voice and feelings matter just as much as theirs. Learning to set boundaries is a courageous step toward self-respect and emotional well-being.

This story highlights the importance of tuning into your own needs. When Lena embraced her individuality through her sketches, she discovered a way to process her feelings and celebrate herself. You can also find a creative outlet—a safe space to express your emotions and connect with your inner self.

It's natural to seek approval from others, but your happiness shouldn't depend on meeting their standards. Lena's decision to speak up for herself wasn't easy, but it was empowering. It shows that being honest about your feelings, even when it's uncomfortable, can lead to deeper understanding and stronger relationships.

Finally, your body and preferences are unique, and that's something to honor, not hide. True confidence comes from accepting who you are, flaws and all, and standing firm in what feels right for you. Like Lena, you can learn to live authentically and embrace the beauty of being true to yourself.

Story 7 - Beyond the Game

From the moment Ella first held a basketball, she knew it was more than just a game—it was a part of her. At fourteen, she spent most of her afternoons on the court, perfecting her free throws, dribbling across the cracked concrete, and pushing herself to get better. Basketball had always been her escape, her haven—a place where she could be her true self without worry. But as tryouts for the school team approached, an unexpected feeling began to settle in—a mix of excitement and unease. This year, she told herself, was the year she'd finally make the team.

Yet, there was another voice, quieter but persistent, that whispered doubts she couldn't ignore. Ella had overheard some of the girls talking in the locker room last season, mentioning that she didn't *"look like a real player"*. *"It's not just about skills; you've got to look right, too."* she'd heard one of them say with a sideways glance. Those words lingered, resurfacing just as she stepped onto the court each day.

But here, standing at the free throw line, those doubts seemed to fade, even if just for a moment.

Ella stood at the free throw line, bouncing the basketball rhythmically as she stared at the hoop. The familiar scuff of the ball against the concrete court and the cool afternoon breeze brushing against her skin were comforting, like a gentle reminder that this place—this game—was hers. She glanced around, watching a few younger kids play nearby, laughing and cheering each other on. Here, on this court, Ella felt alive, like she could let go of everything else and just focus on the game.

"This is where I feel like myself." Ella thought, her fingers instinctively tightening around the ball. *"No expectations. No judgments. Just the game and me."*

Later that week, Ella waited outside the gym doors for the basketball tryouts to start, her stomach flipping with excitement and a tinge of nervousness. She'd practiced all summer, running drills and working on her shots, hoping to secure a spot on the team this year.

As the coach began calling out names for warm-ups, Ella overheard a few teammates talking nearby. Their voices were low, but the words reached her clearly.

"Do you think Ella's really cut out for this? She's got skill, but... you know." one girl muttered, casting a quick glance in Ella's direction.

Another shrugged, *"Coach wants players who look the part, not just play it."*

The words hit Ella harder than she expected, like a chill running through her spine. A thought flickered in her mind—what if they were right?

"Maybe they have a point," she thought, her fingers absentmindedly twisting the hem of her jersey. *"I love basketball, but maybe I don't fit what they're looking for."*

That night, Ella tossed and turned, replaying the conversation in her mind. The excitement of the tryouts was overshadowed by a gnawing doubt she couldn't shake.

The next day, as she walked past the court, she hesitated, the once inviting space now seeming distant and unwelcoming. The thought of stepping onto it felt heavy, and for the first time, she turned away.

"What's the point of trying if they don't think I belong?" Ella thought, gripping her backpack straps tighter. *"Maybe they're right... maybe I just don't have the right look for it."*

The feeling of exclusion and disappointment settled over her like a cloud, making her question if the love she had for basketball was enough.

The following weekend, Ella found herself at her neighborhood community center, quietly shooting hoops on her own. The court felt emptier than usual, like her self-doubt had drained the life out of it. She focused on each bounce of the ball, trying to shake off the nagging thoughts about the tryouts. Just then, Rosa, a local artist and former athlete known for her supportive presence, walked by and paused, watching Ella's focused, determined expression.

"Ella! You've got a great follow-through!" Rosa called with a smile. *"I remember when I used to be glued to this court, just like you."*

Ella gave a faint smile, her shoulders relaxing a bit. *"Thanks, Rosa."* she replied, a bit sheepish. *"Sometimes it feels like this is the only place where I can just be myself, you know?"*

Rosa nodded, her expression softening. *"You know, when I was younger, I was told I didn't 'fit' the sports I loved, either. People said my body wasn't the 'right type' to be a swimmer. I almost let them get in my head."* She paused, meeting Ella's eyes. *"But then I realized my strength wasn't about fitting someone else's picture. It was about how much I loved the water—what I felt when I was doing what I loved. That's where my real strength came from."*

Rosa handed Ella a wristband, engraved with the words: "Strength Comes from Within."

"Wear this as a reminder." Rosa continued, her voice steady and encouraging. *"The people who judge others by looks aren't seeing the*

whole picture. You've got something special, Ella. Don't let anyone make you forget that."

Ella looked down at the wristband, feeling a faint warmth in her chest. For the first time since tryouts, a flicker of hope began to push back against the weight of doubt.

"*Maybe Rosa's right.*" Ella thought, clenching her fist with new resolve. "*I love this game more than anything... Isn't that what should matter?*"

Later that week, Ella made her way back to the gym, the weight of her worries still present, but Rosa's words echoing in her mind. She spotted a group practicing shots on the court, including some of the same teammates who had made her feel out of place. Ella paused, gripping the wristband and taking a deep breath.

She laced up her shoes, walked to the court, and picked up a ball, catching a few surprised glances from the players nearby. Despite the nervous flutter in her stomach, she pushed herself forward, dribbling the ball with purpose.

"*I may not fit what they think a player should look like.*" she thought, her hands finding familiar rhythm with the ball, "*but that doesn't mean I don't belong.*"

With a final, deep breath, Ella squared her shoulders and made her shot, the ball swooshing cleanly through the net. She wasn't here to prove anything to them anymore; she was here for herself, reclaiming the sport she loved.

Ella took one last look at the court as she walked out, Rosa's words still lingering in her mind. *"You've got something special, Ella."* She felt a quiet determination settle within her.

The next morning, she set her alarm early and arrived at the gym just as the sun was rising, the empty court bathed in soft morning light. She took a deep breath, bouncing the ball in the stillness, the sound echoing against the walls. There was no crowd, no pressure—just the rhythm of the game and her heartbeat steadying with each shot she took.

"I'm doing this for me," she thought, feeling the weight of Rosa's wristband warm against her skin. *"I'm here because I love it."*

As she left the gym, a small smile tugged at the corners of her mouth. She'd be back the next morning, ready to give it her all.

Ella's early morning practices quickly became her routine, each dawn marking a fresh chance to work on her skills and remind herself why she loved the game. But at school, the whispers and sidelong glances hadn't disappeared.

But at school, she still faces whispers and sidelong glances. During lunch, she overhears a conversation between teammates, one of whom laughs and says, *"She's working hard, but I don't see still her fitting in with the team. It just doesn't look... right."*

Feeling stung, Ella clenches her tray tighter and heads to an empty table. A classmate, Mia, whom Ella hadn't spoken to much before, notices her alone and decides to sit with her.

Mia sets her tray down and says casually, *"You know, I see you at the gym every morning. Pretty impressive that you're sticking with it."*

Ella gives a half-smile. *"Thanks... I just wish it felt like enough. Sometimes it's hard to tell if I'm even doing this for me or to prove something."*

Mia nods. *"Trust me, I get it. But remember, no one else knows how much this means to you but you. That's what makes it worth doing."*

Through Mia's support, Ella finds a small but meaningful ally — someone who sees her efforts and understands the challenge of staying true to herself amidst external pressures.

With Mia's words resonating in her mind, Ella takes her practice even more seriously, working harder than ever. But as she pushes herself, she feels the weight of judgment building.

One evening, during a practice game, the coach calls her aside.

"*Ella*" the coach starts, not unkindly but with a trace of doubt in his voice. "*I see you're putting in a lot of effort, but this might not be the best fit for you. Basketball requires a certain... look. There's a balance, a... form. Maybe there's another role where you could still support the team?*"

Ella's heart sinks. She forces a nod and turns away, heading to the empty bleachers. The words replay in her mind, an echo of her worst fears.

"*Am I just fooling myself?*" she wonders, gripping the wristband that Rosa gave her. "*I've put in everything I have, but... what if it's still not enough?*"

Feeling lost, Ella sits alone in the gym, looking at the court, which now feels foreign and unwelcoming. This is her lowest point—a moment where she must confront her fear of not measuring up to what others expect of her.

The day after her conversation with the coach, Ella skips practice, avoiding the gym entirely. She wanders aimlessly through town until she finds herself back at the community center, where Rosa is working on a mural.

Rosa notices Ella's troubled expression and invites her over, handing her a paintbrush without asking questions.

Rosa, with her usual calm, says, "*I had a feeling you'd come by. Something's on your mind, isn't it?*"

Ella takes a deep breath. "*They don't think I have the right look. They say I'm not 'built' for basketball. I don't know why I'm even trying anymore.*"

Rosa considers her words before responding. "*Ella, if you love something, you don't need anyone's permission to keep doing it. This isn't about how they see you. This is about how you see yourself. You don't fit a mold because you're creating your own path.*"

Rosa's words settle over Ella like a balm, reigniting a small but fierce spark inside her. For the first time, Ella begins to understand that her value isn't tied to how others perceive her but to the passion she brings to the things she loves.

Ella picks up a brush and begins to paint the mural, creating an image of a lone figure standing strong and defiant against a storm. As she paints, she feels her frustrations flow into each brushstroke, slowly transforming into determination.

Emboldened by her time with Rosa, Ella makes a decision. She won't let others define her worth or tell her where she belongs. The next morning, she heads to the gym with renewed purpose, not to prove anything to others but to reclaim her love for the sport.

During practice, she works with an intensity and confidence that surprises her teammates and even catches the coach's attention. By the end of the session, she's drenched in sweat, her muscles aching, but a genuine smile lights up her face.

"I'm not here to meet anyone's expectations." she thinks as she takes one last shot, watching the ball swish through the net. *"I'm here because I love this game. That's all that matters."*

As she heads off the court, Mia gives her a high-five, and Rosa's wristband feels like a quiet reminder on her wrist: Strength Comes from Within. For the first time, Ella feels a deep sense of satisfaction, knowing that she's on this journey for herself.

Ella leaves the gym that day with a newfound sense of self-worth and purpose. She's no longer chasing approval but rather following her own path, driven by her passion and determination.

After finding newfound confidence in her skills and self-worth, Ella's practices intensify. Her goal is no longer to prove her worth to others but to honor her love for basketball. One afternoon, she's playing alone at the school gym, lost in the rhythm of the ball hitting the court, when the master coach enters.

The master coach watches her for a few moments before speaking up.

"Ella, you've been working hard. I can see the dedication in your game."

Ella pauses, surprised to hear this from him. "Thank you, Coach."

"Listen, we're playing a scrimmage against another school team next week. I'd like to see you out there, giving it your all."

Ella's eyes widen, her heart beating faster. "You mean... you want me to play?"

He nods, a hint of respect in his gaze. *"You've shown more resilience than many others. Let's see what you can do."*

This moment feels surreal to Ella. A few weeks ago, she doubted she'd ever belong on the court again. Now, she's being invited to join. not because her body has changed but because her dedication and skill are undeniable.

Game day arrives, and Ella feels a nervous thrill as she steps onto the court, dressed in her team's colors. The gym is alive with the sounds of sneakers squeaking, cheers echoing, and the buzz of excitement. She knows everyone's watching, but for the first time, she doesn't feel out of place.

As the game begins, Ella's nerves settle. She moves instinctively, her love for basketball guiding her through every pass, dribble, and shot. During a break, she overhears two girls from the opposing team whispering.

"Is that her?" one girl murmurs. *"She doesn't look like the typical player."*

The other girl shrugs. *"Well, she's on the court, isn't she? So, she's got to have something."*

Ella clenches her jaw, but instead of feeling discouraged, she feels a surge of motivation. She realizes that she's no longer defined by these comments; they're just background noise to her love for the game.

"Let them talk" she thinks, her gaze steady on the basket. *"I'm here for myself and for my love of basketball—not to fit into anyone's idea of what I 'should' look like."*

The game is close, with only a few seconds on the clock. Ella catches the ball, and without hesitation, takes a jump shot. The ball arcs perfectly, falling through the hoop as the buzzer sounds. Cheers erupt from her teammates and the audience, and Ella feels a pride that's completely separate from external approval. This is her moment, a victory built on her strength and determination.

As she steps back onto the court, her teammates surround her, patting her on the back and shouting congratulations. One teammate, the very one who had doubted her before, grins and says, *"Ella, that was amazing. I don't know what we would've done without you."*

Ella nods, taking in the moment, but she realizes something surprising: it's not their words that fill her with joy—it's her own. *"I did this,"* she thinks. *"Not to prove anything to them, but because I knew I could."*

Her coach, who once questioned her place on the team, approaches and extends a hand. *"Ella, you showed real heart out there. I underestimated you, and I'm glad you proved me wrong."*

Ella shakes his hand, smiling, but her heart remains steady. She's grateful for the recognition, but she knows she's no longer playing for approval. She's playing for herself, for the love of the game she once nearly walked away from.

Back at home, Ella reflects on her journey, her heart filled with gratitude. She's proud not only of her performance but of the strength she discovered within herself. She pulls out a notebook and begins to write—a mix of feelings and lessons she wants to remember.

"I used to think I had to look a certain way to belong on the court. But I'm realizing that passion and persistence are stronger than any stereotype. I don't have to change to fit anyone's expectations; I just have to stay true to who I am."

As she writes, her thoughts drift to the master coach, Mia, and Rosa—each of whom supported her in different ways. She decides to make her own promise: to never let others' expectations dictate her path.

The next morning, she brings her basketball to the neighborhood community center, where a few younger girls are watching from the sidelines. She smiles at them and tosses one of them the ball.

"You know, you don't have to look any particular way to love this game." she says, nodding with encouragement. *"The only thing that matters is that you love it."*

As Ella watches the girls play, she feels a deep satisfaction, knowing that she's come full circle—not just as a player but as someone who's accepted and embraced her unique journey. She's found her strength, not through changing herself but through reclaiming what she loves and honoring her own strengths.

Learning Lessons from "Beyond the Game"

Ella's story shows that your passion and determination are far more valuable than fitting into someone else's expectations. In a world where people might judge you by appearances or preconceived ideas, it's important to focus on what truly matters: your love for what you do and the effort you bring to it. When Ella chose to honor her passion for basketball, she discovered that her worth was never tied to others' opinions.

You may face moments when self-doubt creeps in, and the words of others make you question yourself. But as Ella learned, your strength comes from within. True confidence doesn't come from trying to meet others' standards—it grows when you embrace your unique qualities and refuse to let judgments define you.

This story also reminds you of the power of resilience. Even when Ella faced rejection and doubt, she didn't give up. By continuing to show up, she reclaimed her place on the court—not by proving herself to others but by reaffirming her own value.

Lastly, Ella's journey teaches the importance of creating your own path. Success is not about fitting into a mold but about staying true to yourself. Like Ella, you have the strength to rise above criticism, honor your passions, and inspire others to do the same.

Story 8 - Roots of Confidence

Mira's bedroom is a blend of her worlds—a colorful woven blanket from her Abuela draped over the bed, walls adorned with pictures of family gatherings, and a small shelf displaying gifts her relatives have brought from visits to their home country. This is where she feels most herself, surrounded by reminders of her heritage. Her Abuela often shares stories of resilience and beauty in their culture, tales that have always made Mira feel proud of who she is.

But recently, things have changed. High school is different, and Mira feels the weight of other people's expectations in a way she never has before. She's caught between the warmth of her cultural roots and the pressure to look like everyone else at school and online. For the first time, she's questioning if she truly belongs in either place.

Mira stands in front of her bedroom mirror, running a finger along the thin braid woven into her hair. It's a small nod to her heritage that her Abuela taught her, but today, Mira feels out of place wearing it. At school, she knows her friends will arrive with sleek, straightened hair, immaculate makeup, and outfits that seem effortlessly "cool" but don't reflect her cultural background.

Mira scrolls through her social media feed and finds the same—models, influencers, and even classmates posting selfies that reinforce a beauty standard that feels impossible for her to meet.

"Why don't I fit in like everyone else?" she thinks, frowning at her reflection. *"If I changed my hair... or my clothes... maybe I wouldn't feel like I'm in two different worlds."*

She tucks a loose strand behind her ear, smoothing out her shirt and heading out the door, still feeling the tug of uncertainty.

At school, Mira sits with her friends in the bustling cafeteria as they talk excitedly about the weekend's big event—a local meet-and-greet with Sofia Carter, an influencer known for her "perfect" looks and her huge social media following. Sofia has become the unofficial standard for beauty among Mira's friends, and the excitement is palpable as they discuss what they'll wear and how they'll style themselves to match her look.

"Can you imagine if we got a selfie with her?" Jess exclaims, her eyes bright.

Lena nods enthusiastically. "I'm planning to try that dewy look she posted last week. She makes it look so easy, but I need to find the right highlighter."

Turning to Mira, Jess grins. "Mira, you should totally come! It'll be fun! And maybe we'll all get a photo with her."

Mira hesitates, glancing down at her lunch. "I don't know... I'm not really into all that. Besides, I'm not sure I'd fit in there."

Jess and Lena share a quick look, a flicker of surprise and slight disappointment crossing their faces. Jess shrugs casually. "Suit yourself, but it would be cool to have you there."

They turn back to their conversation, now diving into tips on matching outfits and Sofia-inspired looks, reinforcing the beauty ideal that Mira feels she lacks. She can't shake the sense of subtle pressure, feeling like an outsider in a conversation that should be lighthearted.

"Maybe if I tried to look more like them, it wouldn't feel like such a big deal," she thinks, feeling the weight of her friends' words. *"But why should I have to change so much?"*

This moment settles heavily with her, solidifying her feeling of inadequacy and pushing her to consider altering her appearance just to feel included in her friends' world.

That evening, Mira stands in front of her bathroom mirror, holding her straightener and staring at her reflection. She's pulled her hair back, imagining it smooth and straight like the influencer she'd seen in countless photos, like her friends wanted for the meet-and-greet. But as she raises the straightener, a pang of discomfort surfaces, and her hand falters.

"Am I really willing to go this far just to fit in?" she wonders, her gaze shifting to the thin braid she's always worn—a piece of her heritage her Abuela had lovingly taught her how to make. The thought begins to deepen, hitting harder. *"My family, my culture... they're part of me. But here I am, trying to erase all of it."*

She sighs, setting the straightener back down. Her chest feels tight, and her mind spins with the weight of the decision. A quiet but resolute feeling starts to stir, questioning whether changing herself so drastically is worth the sense of belonging she hopes to find.

Mira leaves the bathroom, uncertain yet holding onto a flicker of conviction.

The next day, Mira is in her art class with Mrs. Ramirez, her art teacher. Observing that Mira seems quiet, Mrs. Ramirez strikes up a conversation, encouraging her to express her cultural identity through her art.

Mrs. Ramirez: *"You know, Mira, I've seen you put so much heart into your art, but I think there's more of you that's waiting to be expressed."*

Mira: *"I just... I don't feel like the real 'me' fits in here. Sometimes, I wish I could just blend in like everyone else."*

Mrs. Ramirez: *"Fitting in can seem easier, but the world needs your voice, your heritage. Maybe instead of blending in, try letting your art reflect who you really are. There's beauty in diversity, Mira. In being authentically yourself."*

Mrs. Ramirez's words plant a seed of self-worth in Mira. She starts to consider her cultural uniqueness as something valuable rather than a disadvantage. Mira leaves art class feeling lighter, carrying a fresh perspective on her identity and her beauty.

Inspired by Mrs. Ramirez's advice, Mira decides to incorporate small aspects of her culture into her appearance. The next morning, she carefully braids her hair in the traditional style her Abuela taught her, securing it with a gentle touch. She adds a pair of earrings her mother gave her—small hoops adorned with colorful patterns inspired by Latin American art. As she puts them on, Mira pauses, looking at herself in the mirror.

"Maybe it's time I stopped hiding," she thinks, a feeling of quiet confidence beginning to settle. *"These little parts of me—they're beautiful too. They're part of what makes me, me."*

Walking through the school hallway, Mira feels a mix of pride and anxiety. She notices a few curious glances from classmates, but instead of shrinking back, she holds her head a little higher. Though it's a small step, Mira realizes she's crossed an important threshold, taking the first step to reclaim her identity and culture.

With her first small steps toward embracing her cultural roots, Mira feels a budding sense of confidence. But she quickly realizes that holding onto this pride will come with its own set of challenges. As she incorporates these elements into her daily look, Mira braces herself for the reactions she might face from friends and classmates. Soon enough, she encounters the first signs of resistance.

After Mira begins to incorporate small elements of her heritage into her appearance, she feels a renewed sense of pride. But as she walks down the school hallway, a group of classmates gives her curious glances, and one of her peers, Kayla, makes an offhand comment.

Kayla: *"Mira, what's with the new look? Trying something... 'unique'?"*

Mira: *"I thought I'd try something different."*

Kayla: *"Well, it's... definitely different."* She smirks, and Mira senses a tinge of mockery.

Mira feels her confidence waver, her stomach twisting at the judgment in Kayla's voice. She walks away, fighting the impulse to rush to the bathroom and change.

Mira thinks, *"Maybe I'm just making things harder for myself. What if they're right? What if I really do stand out... and not in a good way?"*

Despite this self-doubt, Mira notices her friend, Elena, offering her a supportive smile from across the hall. Elena approaches her and reassures her.

Elena: *"Hey, I love what you're doing with your style. It looks really cool—different in the best way."*

Mira: *"Thanks, Elena. It's hard, you know? I feel like everyone's judging."*

Elena: *"Let them. You're showing them something real. That's more than most people can say."*

Elena's support offers Mira a sense of relief, providing her with a small but meaningful ally.

A few days later, Mira's art teacher, Mrs. Ramirez, assigns a project for students to create self-portraits that capture their inner identity. While some students excitedly chat about their ideas, Mira feels her anxiety rise. She wants to include elements of her cultural heritage, but the pressure to fit Western ideals holds her back.

Sitting at her desk, Mira sketches with tentative strokes, doubting her ability to create a portrait that truly represents her. She considers abandoning the cultural elements altogether and drawing something more conventional.

Mira thinks, *"Maybe I should just play it safe. Do something that won't stand out too much. Why does this have to feel so complicated?"*

This moment highlights Mira's ongoing struggle between expressing her heritage and conforming to mainstream expectations. She feels torn, realizing that embracing her heritage could expose her to more scrutiny.

Mira returns home that evening, discouraged and unsure of how to proceed with her project. Sensing her granddaughter's distress, Mira's Abuela pulls her aside and asks her what's wrong. Mira hesitates, but the warmth in Abuela's eyes encourages her to open up.

Mira: *"Abuela, sometimes I feel like being... me isn't enough. Everyone at school has this 'look,' and I just don't fit."*

Abuela: gently takes Mira's hand *"Mija, you carry so much beauty in you, from our history and culture. Your roots make you strong. You don't need to change to be like anyone else—you're unique as you are."*

Mira: *"But it's hard, Abuela. Sometimes, I feel like if I could just look like everyone else..."*

Abuela: *"Looking like everyone else means hiding the parts of you that make you special. You have something beautiful to share with this world. Don't let anyone make you feel small."*

Her Abuela's words strike a deep chord, reinforcing Mira's value and connection to her cultural heritage. This conversation becomes a turning point, restoring Mira's strength and courage to create her self-portrait in a way that celebrates her identity.

Inspired by her Abuela's words, Mira returns to her sketchbook, determined to embrace her heritage. She starts working on her self-portrait, this time including colors, patterns, and symbols significant to her culture. Her strokes become bolder, capturing both her physical features and her inner identity.

Mira reflects, *"I'm more than just one thing. I'm the music, the stories, the colors. This is who I am. And if others don't get it, that's okay."*

As Mira finishes her portrait, she feels a new sense of pride and connection to herself. The project is no longer just an assignment—it's a declaration of who she is, inside and out.

The following day, she shares her portrait with Mrs. Ramirez, who beams with pride at Mira's work.

Mrs. Ramirez: "Mira, this is beautiful. You've captured something truly powerful. I hope you know how proud you should be."

Mira: smiling *"Thank you. I think I finally see myself... for me."*

This sense of pride and self-recognition represents Mira's initial victory over her insecurities, setting the stage for her journey towards unshakable self-acceptance and resilience.

As Mira's confidence grows, she begins to see her self-portrait as more than just a school project. It's a reflection of her journey, a testament to the parts of herself she once felt compelled to hide. Finishing the final touches on her piece, Mira feels ready to embrace the path she's chosen—one that honors her heritage and her true self.

With her newfound pride, Mira is given the chance to showcase her self-portrait as part of a class project on identity. At first, she hesitates, knowing this means openly sharing her cultural pride—and the artwork she's poured her heart into—with the very people whose opinions once filled her with self-doubt. But she remembers her Abuela's words: *"You have something beautiful to share with this world."*

As the day of her presentation arrives, Mira takes a deep breath, clutching her artwork close to her chest. She knows this isn't just about showing a piece of art—it's about standing in front of her classmates and sharing a side of herself she's fought hard to accept. She can feel her heartbeat quicken, and for a brief moment, the weight of past insecurities resurfaces. But she steadies herself, willing her courage to hold strong, knowing this is her chance to be truly seen.

Mira thinks to herself, *"I know who I am now. I've worked so hard to be able to say that. I'm not hiding anymore."*

When she finally stands before her classmates, she sees some curious glances, a few whispers, but also some nods of quiet encouragement, including from her art teacher and her friend Elena. She presents her piece, explaining how it reflects both her Latina heritage and her personal journey of self-acceptance. The vulnerability is daunting, but it also feels like a release—a freeing moment of truth she's finally ready to share.

Mira: *"For a long time, I thought I had to look a certain way to fit in. But I've started to see that what I see in the mirror isn't just... looks. It's my family, my culture, and everything that makes me, me."*

When she finishes, the room is silent for a moment. Mira feels her heart pounding, unsure of what to expect. Then, she sees a few classmates exchange glances, nodding thoughtfully. Julia, sitting in the front row, breaks the silence.

Julia: (smiling warmly) *"Wow, Mira, that's really amazing. I never thought about things like that."*

Sofia, a usually quiet classmate, chimes in, her voice soft but sincere.

Sofia: *"Yeah, it's... like a whole different way to look at yourself."*

Mira looks around and catches a few more approving nods. She notices Kayla, one of her tougher critics from earlier, actually looking impressed, her gaze softened. The art teacher, Mrs. Ramirez, gives her a proud smile and a small thumbs-up.

A few more classmates speak up with words of support, and Mira feels a weight lift, replaced by a growing warmth. For the first time, she senses real acceptance—not just of her story, but of the real her.

Mira thinks, *"Maybe sharing my story did more than I thought. Maybe... it opened something up for everyone here, too."*

With her heart full, Mira walks back to her seat, a sense of belonging settling over her. She feels lighter, as though the weight of her story has been shared with everyone in the room. It's no longer just her journey; somehow, it feels like her classmates now carry a piece of it, understanding her in a way she'd never imagined possible.

In the days that follow her presentation, Mira notices a profound shift within herself. She feels an unshakeable confidence in her heritage and appearance, no longer measuring herself against others. When she looks at herself in the mirror, she doesn't think about fitting into a single standard. Instead, she sees a complete, unique individual— someone defined not by comparisons, but by her own spirit and experiences.

One afternoon, while scrolling through social media, she sees a post featuring the very ideals she once aspired to. But now, she feels no pressure to conform; instead, she feels pride in her own unique path.

Mira thinks, *"I'm finally at peace. I don't need to look like anyone else because I bring my own beauty, my own story. And that's enough."*

This newfound clarity marks her complete transformation. She knows that this confidence won't fade—she's finally grounded in her own identity.

Having completed her journey of self-discovery, Mira becomes a quiet yet powerful inspiration among her classmates and friends. Her confidence in her identity encourages others to embrace their own uniqueness, sparking small but noticeable shifts in those around her. She sees classmates subtly incorporating symbols of their heritage— bracelets, earrings, or hairstyles—as if, for the first time, they're finding the courage to show more of who they really are.

One day at lunch, her friend Elena joins her, beaming as they talk about the impact Mira's presentation has had on others.

Elena: *"You know, people really noticed what you shared. It's like it gave them permission to think about their own roots."*

Mira: *smiling* "*I used to worry so much about what everyone thought. I never realized that by just being myself, I could help others feel okay with who they are, too.*"

Elena: "*You're showing them that they don't have to fit in to feel... complete.*"

As Mira watches her friends laughing, each of them carrying their own story and uniqueness, a deep sense of peace and fulfillment washes over her. For the first time, she feels that her journey has touched more lives than just her own.

"This journey was never about changing to meet anyone else's expectations," Mira thinks. "It was about finally seeing myself as whole—and inspiring others to see their own wholeness, too."

Learning Lessons from Roots of Confidence

Mira's journey shows that staying true to yourself is a powerful act of courage. It can be tempting to change who you are to fit into the mold that others expect of you, but Mira's story reminds you that your individuality—your roots, your culture, and your experiences—are what make you beautiful and strong.

When Mira began to embrace her heritage, she discovered a deeper connection to herself. You don't need to erase the unique parts of who you are to belong. Instead, honor your identity and remember that your voice matters. Others may not always understand, but authenticity will always feel more rewarding than hiding parts of yourself.

Mira's story also highlights the importance of finding allies who see your worth. Whether it's a friend, a teacher, or a family member, these people can remind you of your strengths and help you push past self-doubt.

Finally, Mira learned that confidence grows when you stop comparing yourself to others and start celebrating your own story. By choosing to express her cultural roots, Mira inspired her classmates and proved that authenticity has the power to break down barriers. You, too, can inspire others by embracing your unique journey—and in doing so, you'll find that you've always been enough.

Story 9 - Unfolding Confidence

Lina's room was her sanctuary—a quiet retreat where she could lose herself in her drawings and escape the noise of the outside world. She loved the feeling of pencil against paper, watching as her sketches slowly came to life. In this private space, surrounded by her favorite art supplies and stacks of well-worn books, Lina felt most like herself: calm, focused, and unbothered by the expectations she encountered at school.

She wasn't someone who fussed over her appearance or sought attention. She kept mostly to herself, her interests and talents known only to her closest friends. At school, blending in was effortless—her jeans and T-shirts went unnoticed, her days passing quietly and predictably.

But today, as Lina settled into her bed with her sketchbook open on her lap, a soft buzz interrupted her thoughts. Her phone screen lit up with a notification. She glanced at it, her heart skipping as she saw the photo: a candid shot of Ethan, the boy who had lately made her pulse quicken. He was laughing with friends at a school event, looking effortlessly confident, the kind of confidence that seemed out of reach for someone like her.

She set her sketchbook aside, unable to resist the pull to look closer. She felt a pang of self-awareness as she caught her reflection in the mirror across her room. For the first time, she wondered what he might see if he looked her way, if he'd notice her among the many faces that drifted through the hallways.

"*I wonder if he even notices girls like me.*" she thought, her gaze lingering on her reflection. "*Girls who don't have that perfectly put-together look.*"

The room that had always felt safe and complete suddenly seemed smaller, like it didn't quite hold everything she wanted for herself anymore.

The next day, Lina found herself drifting through the noise of the school cafeteria, her gaze unconsciously drawn to the table where Ethan and his friends sat. She couldn't hear every word, but snippets floated her way, catching her attention. Ethan was laughing with his friends, his voice animated as he spoke about the kind of girl he admired—someone "confident and cool." A girl who knew how to carry herself, who seemed effortlessly put together.

Lina's heart sank just a little as she took it all in, the feeling settling heavy and unfamiliar in her chest. She glanced down at her T-shirt and jeans, noticing the frayed edges and the ink smudge on her sleeve from last night's sketching. The girl Ethan described didn't look anything like her. But, somehow, for the first time, she wanted to.

Across the table, her friends chatted and laughed, oblivious to her distraction until her friend Sarah nudged her with a smirk.

"*Earth to Lina! You're zoning out on us again. What's up?*" Sarah teased, raising an eyebrow.

Lina blinked, her face heating up as she realized she'd been staring. "*Oh, nothing... Just thinking.*" she replied, trying to shake off the strange new feeling gnawing at her.

But as she glanced back at Ethan, the thought persisted, louder and more insistent.

"Maybe if I looked more like those girls—more confident, more put together—he'd actually notice me." she mused, her stomach twisting.

A subtle shift had begun within her, a quiet whisper urging her to fit a mold she hadn't even realized existed in her world until now.

That evening, Lina lay on her bed, scrolling through her social media feed, her thumb pausing on each polished image of girls from her school. Their photos felt like scenes from a magazine—styled hair, carefully curated outfits, confident poses. Each picture seemed to shout a confidence she suddenly felt she lacked.

Her fingers tightened around her phone, her heart heavy with a strange new doubt. Without thinking, she set the phone aside and reached for her sketchbook, feeling its worn cover beneath her fingertips. It was a familiar comfort, a place where she could express herself without worrying about how others saw her.

She flipped it open, but instead of drawing, she found herself staring blankly at the page, her mind turning back to Ethan's words. The image of herself, effortlessly confident, maybe just a little different—enough to catch his eye—floated into her mind.

"Am I really willing to go this far just to fit in?" she wondered, feeling a pang of uncertainty. *"Isn't there more to me than just looks?"* She tapped her pencil absently on the page. *"But... what if he never sees me as interesting if I stay like this?"*

Her heart twisted with the question, leaving her torn. The part of her that found joy in her art, in the quiet strength of just being herself, clashed with the newer, unfamiliar desire for acceptance. With a sigh, she closed her sketchbook, its pages a reminder of who she was beneath the surface—a reminder she wasn't sure she was ready to let go of.

One afternoon, Lina lingered in the art room after class, her gaze drawn to the unfinished projects and vibrant paintings lining the walls. The golden afternoon light filtered in, casting a warm glow over the tables cluttered with paintbrushes, pastels, and blank canvases—all waiting to become something more.

Ms. Foster, her art teacher, approached with a kind smile. "*Lina, could you give me a hand with these supplies?*" she asked, motioning to a jumble of paints. Lina nodded, grateful for a quiet moment to distract her from the tangled thoughts about herself and her place in the world.

As they organized the shelves in companionable silence, Ms. Foster glanced at her with a knowing look. "*You know, I used to struggle a lot in high school, too. I thought I needed to fit in perfectly to be liked or respected.*" She paused, the hint of a memory softening her expression. "*But over time, I realized that the people who see the real you—the people who matter—they'll notice you for who you are, not for who you pretend to be.*"

Lina hesitated, running a finger over a bright palette of colors. "*But what if... I'm too plain to stand out?*" she murmured, the words slipping out before she could hold them back. "*It feels like people only notice you if you look like everyone else.*"

Ms. Foster handed Lina a brush, her expression warm and thoughtful. "*Lina, true confidence isn't about becoming someone else. It's about understanding that you already have everything that makes you remarkable, just as you are. And when you believe that, others will see it too.*"

As she took in Ms. Foster's words, Lina felt a spark of something she couldn't quite name—a gentle reassurance she hadn't known she needed. Her eyes drifted to the jars of paint, the vibrant colors reminding her of the sketches she'd kept hidden away, the ones that felt like pieces of herself. Could embracing her own colors be enough?

"*She makes it sound so easy.*" Lina thought, the weight of doubt still lingering. "*But... maybe there's something to what she's saying.*"

For the first time in days, Lina felt a quiet sense of hope, as if she were finally seeing a glimpse of herself in a new light, surrounded by the colors and textures of the art room—a place where authenticity was valued over imitation.

Encouraged by Ms. Foster's words about staying true to herself, Lina decides to make a subtle but meaningful shift. Instead of scrutinizing every detail of her appearance, she focuses on how she feels—comfortable and like herself. In the morning, as she stands in front of her mirror, she resists the urge to fuss over her look. Instead, she braids her hair in her favorite practical style and pulls on her most comfortable hoodie, the one that feels like a hug. She then reaches for her sketchbook. For the first time in a while, she feels a quiet excitement about bringing it along.

Pausing, Lina glances at her reflection, noticing a calmness she hadn't felt in days.

*"Maybe I don't need to change myself to stand out. Maybe...
being me is enough to start with."*

At school, her friends give her a quick once-over, but she meets their glances with a steady, quiet confidence. As she walks down the hallway, a few people give her curious looks, but she holds her sketchbook tighter, its familiar weight grounding her.

In art class, Ms. Foster notices her choice to bring her sketchbook and gives her a small, encouraging nod—a silent acknowledgment of Lina's first step toward self-acceptance. Sitting down, Lina opens her sketchbook and begins drawing, feeling more like herself than she has in a long time.

Across the table, her classmate Zoe notices her sketches and say to her: *"I didn't know you drew like that, Lina. That's really cool."*

Lina, smiling shyly but feeling proud: *"Thanks... it's just something I enjoy."*

As she continues to draw, Lina realizes that this small choice—showing up as herself—is a powerful beginning. And maybe, just maybe, it's enough.

With her first step toward embracing her authentic self, Lina enters the school hallway, wearing an outfit that feels comfortable and more reflective of her style—soft colors, loose jeans, her favorite hoodie. Her sketchbook is tucked under her arm, a quiet symbol of her commitment to bringing more of herself into her daily life. The previous night, she had felt a growing sense of confidence, but now, as she catches glimpses of judgmental stares, that confidence wavers.

As she walks, a couple of girls nearby notice her change. They share a look before one of them smirks and walks up to her.

Ava: *"New look, Lina? Trying to go for that 'artist vibe' or something?"*

Lina: *"Yeah... I just wanted to bring a bit more of myself to school, I guess."*

Ava: *"Well... it's definitely different."*

Ava's words linger, and Lina's confidence dips. She feels her cheeks heat up as her self-doubt begins to creep in, and she tightens her grip on her sketchbook.

Lina's thoughts raced: *"Do I really stand out this much... and is that a bad thing? Why should it matter what they think? This is supposed to be about me, not them."*

Just then, her friend Katie appears from across the hall. She spots Lina's expression and, noticing Ava walking away, gives Lina a reassuring smile.

Katie: *"Hey, Lina! I love what you're doing—it really suits you. Don't mind people like Ava."*

Lina: *"Thanks, Katie. Sometimes... I'm not even sure if I'm doing this for me or if I'm just trying to prove something to everyone else."*

Katie: *"Maybe it's a little of both, and that's okay. Just remember, there's so much more to you than what they see."*

Katie's words bring a sense of calm to Lina, allowing her to focus on why she began this journey. Buoyed by her friend's encouragement, Lina walks to her next class feeling a renewed resolve, carrying her sketchbook openly, as a reminder to herself that she can trust her own choices.

The school courtyard was buzzing with the usual chatter, friends gathered in clusters laughing and talking about weekend plans. Lina had found a quiet corner to sketch, focusing on capturing the shadows cast by the trees and letting herself relax into her art. But then she looked up, catching sight of Ethan across the courtyard.

He was laughing with Madison, a girl in her grade known for her polished look and effortless style. Madison had this way of moving, confident and casual, that made her seem so at ease with herself. And as Lina watched, she felt a pang she hadn't felt in a while—a mix of longing and self-doubt. Madison's hair seemed to shine in the sunlight, her outfit perfectly coordinated. And there was Ethan, captivated by her, hanging on to her every word.

Lina's heart sank as she observed them, her gaze dropping back to her sketchbook. She couldn't help but think of the efforts she'd made recently to stay true to herself. But here was the reality: Ethan didn't seem to notice or care. He was drawn to someone else, someone who looked nothing like her, and suddenly all her self-assurance felt like it was slipping through her fingers.

"Maybe I'll never be the type of girl he notices," Lina thought, closing her sketchbook with a sigh. *"She's everything I'm not. Why does this have to feel so hard? Maybe being myself just... isn't enough."*

For the first time since she'd started her journey, Lina felt the pull to change again, to mold herself into what she thought Ethan—and maybe everyone else—wanted. Her confidence in being her true self felt fragile, like a candle flickering in a breeze, and she was afraid it might go out altogether.

Yet even as she sat there, wrestling with her doubt, she felt a small resistance within—a voice that reminded her of her recent progress, of the quiet pride she'd been building. This voice was faint, almost hidden beneath her insecurities, but it was there, urging her to remember why she'd started this journey. And although she couldn't fully silence her doubt, she decided, at least for now, to leave that courtyard without altering herself.

But the test was becoming harder, and she knew the real challenge was still ahead.

The night of the school social arrived, and Lina stood in front of her bedroom mirror, almost not recognizing herself. She wore a trendy, tight dress her friends had urged her to buy, along with heavy makeup that felt foreign on her face. Staring at her reflection, she fidgeted with her mom's bracelet, feeling torn. *"Am I really going to throw away everything just to fit in tonight? But maybe this is what it takes for people to notice me. Maybe it's what it'll take for Ethan to notice me..."*

Taking a deep breath, she headed to the event, hoping her outfit would give her the confidence she craved. But almost immediately, she felt uncomfortable—her dress too tight, her makeup too thick. She spotted Ethan laughing with a group of friends, including a few classmates who looked at ease, effortlessly themselves.

He didn't glance her way, completely engrossed in the natural, joyful energy of the people around him. Watching them, Lina realized that none of them seemed concerned with "perfect looks" or meeting anyone's expectations; they were simply enjoying the night.

In that moment, clarity washed over her. *"He's not paying attention to my dress or makeup,"* she thought. *"He's having fun with people who are just being real."*

Feeling a rush of relief, Lina slipped into the bathroom and faced her reflection. She looked at the heavy makeup and dress, realizing how far she'd gone to be someone she wasn't. *"This isn't me. I shouldn't have to change myself to be noticed."*

With a sense of resolve, she wiped off her makeup, tied her hair back, and felt the weight of pretense lift. When she stepped back into the event, it wasn't for anyone's approval; it was to enjoy herself, just as she was.

After the school event, Lina felt different—clearer and more grounded. She returned to school the next day wearing her favorite comfortable sweater, her hair pulled back naturally, and her sketchbook tucked under her arm. For the first time, she didn't wonder what others might think; she simply felt herself.

Walking down the hallway, she noticed her friend Katie heading her way, eyes lighting up when she saw her.

Katie: *"Lina, there's something different about you today. You look... like you. But, I don't know, more confident?"*

Lina: *"Thanks, Katie. I just realized that if someone doesn't appreciate me as I am, then maybe they're not my people."*

Katie nodded approvingly, and Lina felt a rush of gratitude for her friend's support.

As she continued down the hall, Lina caught her reflection in the window, and for the first time, she felt proud of what she saw. She didn't need anyone's approval or praise. Just walking through those hallways, knowing she was being true to herself, was a reward in itself.

"Being myself is enough. It always has been."

Back in her room at home, Lina sat at her desk, staring at a blank journal page. Her English teacher had assigned a project about identity, something deeply personal that could be shared with the class. The assignment felt like a chance to be real, to show how much she'd grown. But the thought of sharing her recent struggles—the insecurity, the need for others' approval, and the self-discovery that followed—was daunting.

The question lingered: should she keep it safe and surface-level, or let her classmates see the real her? Her fingers hovered over her pen, hesitation tugging at her.

Lina glanced at her reflection in the nearby mirror, the same reflection she'd scrutinized just weeks ago. Now, she saw someone with a story worth telling, a story that might resonate with others.

"If I share this.." she thought, *"maybe someone else will feel less alone. Maybe they'll see that it's okay to be exactly who they are."*

Taking a deep breath, Lina picked up her pen, letting her thoughts pour onto the page. She wrote about the desire to fit in, the struggle of feeling like she constantly fell short, and the realization that real confidence came from embracing her true self. When she finished, she read the title: "Learning to Embrace Myself."

For Lina, this project became more than a school assignment—it was a testament to her journey and a step toward owning her story.

The day of Lina's presentation arrives, and though her hands tremble slightly, she stands at the front of the classroom, determined. As she reads aloud, her initial nerves begin to ease, replaced by a sense of quiet strength she hadn't expected. With every line, Lina shares the journey from self-doubt to self-acceptance, feeling pride with each word.

When she finishes, the room is silent. A few classmates nod in quiet understanding, and Katie gives her an encouraging smile from the back row.

Jenna: *"Lina, that was brave. I had no idea you felt like that. I think a lot of us do."*

Dylan: *"It's cool you're just... being you. Makes me think about how much I change to fit in too."*

As Lina looks around, her initial fear dissolves. *"Maybe sharing my story helped others realize they don't have to change to feel valued,"* she thinks, feeling a sense of connection and purpose.

Her journey has inspired her classmates, showing them that true worth comes from being who they are, without trying to fit someone else's mold.

In the days after her presentation, Lina feels a calm confidence she's never known. Her classmates look at her a little differently now, with a sense of respect she hadn't expected. At lunch, she's heading to her usual table when she notices Ethan walking toward her, looking a bit hesitant.

Lina's heart skips as Ethan stops in front of her, shuffling his feet a little, his usual easy confidence softened.

Ethan: *"Hey, Lina... I just wanted to say that your presentation was... really brave. I mean, it's cool that you shared so much of yourself. It kind of made me think about... well, I guess just being honest with myself too."*

Lina: *"Thanks, Ethan. I never thought sharing my story could actually... help anyone else."*

Ethan: *"It did. A lot of us could never say the stuff you did."*

As Ethan walks off, Lina feels a warmth settle in her chest, deeper than the thrill of a simple compliment. Her presentation wasn't just a milestone for her—it resonated with others, too. She realizes now that she's not only found a new respect for herself but maybe has helped others, like Ethan, see the strength in being real.

Lina thought to herself, *"This journey wasn't about changing for anyone. It was about learning to honor who I am—and maybe helping others do the same."*

This moment marks her quiet triumph, her elixir: the knowledge that by being true to herself, she has inspired her peers to think about their own paths toward self-acceptance.

Learning Lessons from "Unfolding Confidence"

Lina's journey reminds us that true confidence comes from within, not from conforming to external expectations. It's easy to feel the pressure to change who you are to gain approval or fit into someone else's idea of perfection, but Lina's story shows the power of embracing your authentic self.

Her struggle with self-doubt, fueled by comparisons and the desire for acceptance, is something many teens face. Lina's breakthrough comes when she realizes that her worth isn't tied to looking a certain way or being noticed by others. Instead, it lies in recognizing the value of her unique qualities—her creativity, her quiet strength, and her genuine nature.

This story also highlights the importance of surrounding yourself with people who uplift you. Supportive friends, mentors, and allies, like Katie and Ms. Foster, remind us that we don't have to face challenges alone. They help Lina see that self-acceptance doesn't mean being perfect; it means celebrating the imperfect, real parts of yourself.

Ultimately, Lina learns that authenticity not only empowers her but also inspires others. By choosing to stay true to herself, she paves the way for her classmates to reflect on their own insecurities and embrace their individuality. You, too, can find strength in being yourself—because your story is worth sharing, just as it is.

Story 10 - True Style

Early in her teens, Nadia lives in the familiar rhythm of school, time with her small group of friends, and her creative escape—jewelry-making. At home, her jewelry kit is her sanctuary, a place where she can lose herself in designing pieces that reflect her personality. Each bead and charm she strings together feels like an extension of her inner world, and she imagines wearing her creations with pride.

But at school, Nadia's world feels restrictive. Most of her friends gravitate toward the latest fashion trends and wear the popular fitted jeans, crop tops, and accessories that are all over social media. Nadia doesn't feel like she can pull off those looks with the same ease. Instead, she sticks to her loose hoodies and jeans, choosing comfort but at the cost of feeling a bit... invisible.

On a Saturday afternoon, Nadia sits cross-legged on her bedroom floor, flipping through a fashion magazine she borrowed from her friend. The pages are filled with trendy outfits that make her feel a mix of admiration and frustration. She sets the magazine aside and picks up a charm bracelet she's been working on, adding beads that match her favorite colors. She glances at her reflection in the mirror, holding the bracelet up against her wrist, and pictures herself wearing it confidently in front of her friends. But that thought quickly fades, leaving her with the familiar tug of doubt.

"Why can't I feel as put together as they do? Maybe if I looked more like that, I'd feel like I belong."

On Monday, as Nadia steps into the bustling cafeteria, she catches the lively conversation between her friends. They're excitedly discussing the upcoming school dance, talking about what they plan to wear, how they'll do their hair, and how the dance's theme is inspiring their outfits. One friend eagerly pulls out her phone, showing off a picture of the shimmering dress she's chosen.

Emma: "Nadia! Have you thought about what you're wearing? You always make those amazing bracelets and earrings. You could totally create something unique!"

Nadia: "Oh, um... I haven't really thought about it yet."

Emma: "You should go all out! We're all going to look amazing. Don't hold back!"

As Lily and Emma's laughter and chatter fill the air, a mix of emotions swirls within Nadia. Part of her feels that this dance could be an opportunity to express herself—an invitation to showcase the creativity she usually keeps hidden. But with that excitement comes a familiar worry, a whisper of doubt about how she'll measure up if she dares to stand out.

Nadia thinks to herself, *"What if I go for something different and it doesn't look right? Or worse... what if I don't fit in at all? Maybe it's better to play it safe."*

Later that evening, Nadia finds herself alone in her room, the quiet bringing her friends' excitement back to mind. Their encouragement lingers, but self-doubt overshadows it, clouding her enthusiasm. She sits at her desk, glancing over at the bracelets and earrings she's crafted—unique pieces she's always been proud of but never dared to wear to something like a school dance. Beside her, a small sketchbook lies open to a design she sketched earlier: a colorful layered skirt paired with a top she could personalize with her favorite accessories.

She lifts the page and studies it in the dim light, feeling a tug of longing mixed with anxiety.

Nadia thinks, *"Am I really brave enough to wear this? What if it just looks... wrong? Or worse... what if I look completely out of place?"*

She sighs, her fingers tracing over the edges of the sketch. The idea of wearing something bold suddenly feels too risky, the imagined reactions of others echoing in her mind. With a heavy sigh, Nadia folds the page and tucks it deep into her notebook, out of sight. Maybe playing it safe is better. She resolves to pick something familiar—something that won't make her stand out.

Nadia shuts the notebook, turning away from her creativity, if only for a moment, choosing the comfort of blending in over the fear of standing out.

The next day, Nadia's art teacher, Ms. Monroe, catches her at the end of class. Ms. Monroe has always been someone Nadia admires—her effortless style and bold, creative approach to life make her stand out, not just to her students but in every room she enters. She's noticed Nadia's hesitation recently and gently encourages her, often complimenting her unique taste in handmade accessories.

As the classroom empties and a comfortable quiet settles over them, Ms. Monroe sets aside her brush, giving Nadia an encouraging smile.

Ms. Monroe: *"Nadia, you've seemed a little quieter than usual. Is something on your mind?"*

Nadia looks down, twisting one of her bracelets. *"I just... feel like no matter what I try, I don't quite fit in. It's like I'll never have the right look. Sometimes it's easier to just hide."*

Ms. Monroe nods thoughtfully. *"You know, I used to feel the same way."* she says, a gentle warmth in her voice. *"I thought I had to dress* and act a certain way for people to notice me. But then I realized—style is meant to show people who you are, not to match anyone else."*

Nadia feels a twinge of doubt mixed with a spark of hope. *"She makes it sound so easy, she thinks, Maybe there's something to what she's saying... but could I actually pull that off?"*

Ms. Monroe gives her a soft nudge. *"Nadia, true confidence comes when you're comfortable in your own skin. Start with something small that feels true to you. You might be surprised by what happens."*

Nadia leaves the classroom feeling a flicker of possibility. Ms. Monroe's words stay with her, and for the first time, she considers what it might feel like to wear something that truly reflects her own style—not anyone else's.

The night after her talk with Ms. Monroe, Nadia feels an urge to make a change. She opens her wardrobe and scans through her clothes, her eyes landing on a colorful scarf she'd made over the summer. It's not trendy or something her friends would choose, but it's hers—her design, her colors, her creation. Nadia holds it for a moment, hearing Ms. Monroe's words echo in her mind, reminding her that true style reflects who you are.

The next morning, Nadia stands in front of her mirror, slowly draping the scarf around her shoulders, adjusting it just so. It feels bold, like a part of herself she's hidden too long. Her heart skips as she imagines walking into school with something so different from what her friends wear, but she steels herself.

"Okay," she thinks, *"it's just a scarf... but it's mine. Maybe this is a start."*

With one last look in the mirror, Nadia takes a deep breath, lifts her chin, and steps out of her room, feeling a small, new spark of confidence as she heads out the door.

With her new scarf—a small but meaningful attempt at expressing herself—Nadia feels a glimmer of confidence. But at school, the response is not what she'd hoped for. As she walks through the crowded hallway, she notices quick glances, a few whispers, and catches herself wondering if wearing the scarf was the right choice.

Nadia heads to her locker, clutching her books a little tighter when she overhears a classmate, *Emily*, snickering nearby with her friend. Emily looks over, giving Nadia's scarf an exaggerated once-over.

Emily: *"New look, Nadia? Trying to, like, make a statement or something?"*

Nadia: *"Just thought I'd try something different."*

Emily: *"Well... it's different, alright."* Emily smirks and walks away, leaving Nadia feeling more exposed than she expected.

Just then, her friend *Ava* steps forward, catching Nadia's eye with a gentle smile.

Ava: *"Hey, I love the scarf. It's really... you."*

Nadia: *"Thanks, Ava. It's just—sometimes, trying to be 'me' feels like the hardest thing."*

In this moment, Nadia faces her first real test, confronted with the judgment of others. But Ava's support reminds her that not everyone sees her unique style as "too different." And though her confidence wavers, the quiet encouragement helps her feel she isn't completely alone.

As Nadia watches Emily walk away, a thought tugs at her, *"Why does being myself have to feel so difficult? Maybe if I could just blend in like Emily, things would be easier. But... is that even what I want?"*

This small trial forces Nadia to ask herself what truly matters—fitting in or expressing who she really is—and she begins to realize that perhaps standing out is worth the risk.

Later that week, Nadia finds herself at a friend's house for a small gathering. She'd hesitated to come, wondering if her style would stand out too much, but decided to join in anyway. As she walks into the living room, she notices Jason chatting easily with a few friends near the window. Nadia's heart sinks as she takes in how effortlessly her friends seem to embody the trends she feels outside of—polished, fashionable, and composed.

Nadia shifts by the door, adjusting the scarf she'd chosen to wear, a piece she'd once felt proud of. But now, in this setting, surrounded by people who seem to fit so seamlessly into what's "expected," her scarf suddenly feels like a spotlight, an emblem of how out of place she feels. She watches as Emily, wearing the latest fashion, engages Jason in conversation, her confidence seeming to light up the room. Nadia takes a deep breath, suddenly unsure of herself and wondering if she even belongs.

As Nadia stands there, a thought crosses her mind. *"Maybe I'll never be the kind of girl who fits in without trying. Why do I have to feel so different? The more I try to be myself, the more I feel like an outsider."*

In this tense moment, Nadia feels the pull to conform intensify. She stands on the edge of a decision, tempted to abandon her style in favor of blending in, doubting whether staying true to herself is worth feeling like she's on the outside.

As Nadia prepares to attend a family gathering that evening, her mom encourages her to dress comfortably, reminding her that she doesn't need to impress anyone. However, with nerves creeping in about being compared to her fashion-forward cousin, Maya, Nadia hesitates. Her first instinct is to wear something trendy and safe, like the styles her friends typically choose.

But after a pause, she decides to embrace her individuality, choosing an outfit she once sketched in her notebook—a flowing dress paired with her favorite cardigan and her signature scarf.

Nadia steps into her aunt's house, feeling a mix of pride and vulnerability in her unique outfit. Her eyes scan the room until she spots Maya and her cousins by the snack table. Maya, impeccably dressed and surrounded by compliments, glances over, and Nadia catches her faint smirk.

Maya: *"Well, Nadia, I see you're still experimenting. Scarves, huh? Didn't know those were a thing again."*

Nadia's stomach drops, her fingers instinctively reaching for the scarf. The sting of Maya's words settles deep, and the urge to conform tugs at her resolve.

Nadia looks toward her reflection in a nearby window. *"Why does her opinion hit so hard? I chose this because I love it. Why should I need Maya's approval to feel like myself?"*

Taking a slow, calming breath, Nadia straightens her shoulders and lets her hand fall from the scarf, choosing not to hide. She catches her mom's proud smile from across the room, an unspoken reminder of her journey toward self-expression.

In this moment, Nadia's confidence is both challenged and strengthened, marking a turning point in her commitment to staying true to herself. Rather than succumbing to Maya's judgment, she finds a deeper sense of resilience within, realizing that her self-worth doesn't need validation from anyone else.

Having stood her ground at the family gathering, Nadia wakes up the next morning with a newfound sense of freedom. She feels lighter, almost as if shedding the need for others' approval has given her permission to truly express herself. That day, she selects an outfit that combines elements of her own style—bold earrings she made herself, her favorite patterned scarf, and a shirt she's always loved but felt too shy to wear. With a deep breath and a growing sense of pride, Nadia heads to school, feeling more like herself than ever.

At lunch, Nadia walks over to the cafeteria table, where Ava and Sarah immediately notice her outfit.

Ava: *"Nadia, you look amazing! That scarf suits you so well—it's totally you."*

Sarah: *"Yeah, seriously. I always thought you had the best accessories, but you never wore them. Seeing you wear your style so confidently... it's kind of inspiring."*

Nadia: *"Thanks, guys. I think I finally realized that I don't have to fit into a trend or anyone else's idea of what's 'in'—it's way more meaningful to wear what makes me feel good."*

As her friends admire her unique style, Nadia realizes that her authenticity has a positive impact beyond herself. For the first time, she understands that expressing her individuality can inspire others to do the same, and she feels her self-confidence radiate in a way she hadn't expected.

As Nadia considers how far she's come, a thought settles in, clear and certain: *"Maybe this is what real confidence feels like—not shrinking or changing for others, but being true to myself. And maybe, just maybe, that's exactly where I'm meant to be."*

In this moment, Nadia embraces the reward of her journey: a sense of self-worth rooted in her own choices and style, inspiring others to find the same courage.

With her newfound confidence and individuality, Nadia has been embracing her unique style. One afternoon, her English teacher, Ms. Roberts, announces a project on self-expression and identity, asking students to create something that represents who they are. At first, Nadia hesitates—sharing her journey feels vulnerable, and she's unsure if she's ready to reveal such a personal part of herself to her classmates. But as she thinks about it, she realizes that this project could be her chance to step fully into the person she's become and celebrate the path she's taken.

That night in her bedroom, Nadia sits at her desk, her favorite pens and markers laid out around her, sketchbook open. She starts to outline an art piece that combines her love for fashion with her journey toward self-acceptance. The page slowly fills with sketches of different body shapes, styles, and colors, a celebration of personal expression and diversity.

She pauses, glancing over the artwork, feeling a surge of both pride and doubt.

"Am I really ready to put this out there for everyone to see? But... maybe this is exactly what I need—to own my story and show that I'm proud of who I am."

With a deep breath, she leans back, feeling a sense of purpose solidify within her. She decides to title her piece *"True Style"*—a reflection of her journey and a tribute to all the things that make her feel authentically herself.

When the day finally arrives for Nadia to present her project, she feels a mix of nerves and quiet excitement. Standing before her class, she holds up her collage—a blend of sketches, colors, and designs celebrating individuality and unique style. Her heart races as she explains the journey behind it, sharing her struggle with self-image and how she discovered that fashion could be a personal expression of identity rather than a standard she had to fit.

The classroom falls silent as Nadia speaks, her voice growing stronger with each word. She takes a steadying breath, glancing at her collage and then at her classmates. She talks about how embracing her own style helped her feel more like herself. When she finishes, she glances around and notices her friend Ava beaming proudly. Even Emma, who once made her question herself, looks unexpectedly thoughtful.

Lily: *"Nadia, that was amazing. I never really thought of style as a way to show who you are. I just thought it was about keeping up with trends."*

Samira: *"It's inspiring. You've made me wonder why I spend so much energy worrying about what everyone else thinks. I love how you're making fashion your own thing."*

As Nadia listens to her classmates' reactions, a warm feeling stirs within her—a blend of pride and relief. *"Maybe I did more than just share my project. Maybe... I helped them see that it's okay to be themselves too."*

Her initial fears fade, replaced by a deep sense of connection and fulfillment. Sharing her story has inspired others to reflect on their own self-expression, and Nadia realizes that her journey might just be encouraging others to embrace their own unique styles.

After her presentation, Nadia senses a quiet but profound change within herself. The weight of seeking others' approval feels lighter, replaced by a steady confidence born from embracing her unique style. During lunch, she's seated with her friend Ava when Jonah, a classmate she's always admired for his easygoing confidence, walks up to her with a genuine smile.

Nadia and Ava are laughing over something trivial when Jonah approaches, looking slightly self-conscious but genuinely interested.

"Hey, Nadia" he begins, a bit shyly. *"I wanted to say I thought your project was really inspiring. It… it kind of made me think about how much I try to fit in, even if it doesn't feel right sometimes. You really showed us something different."*

Nadia feels warmth spread through her, his words sinking in. *"Thank you, Jonah."* she says, smiling. *"I think I finally realized that it's way more fulfilling to be yourself than to blend in for someone else's approval."*

Jonah nods, clearly impressed, and heads back to his table, leaving Nadia with a sense of validation she didn't expect—but not from blending in; rather, from standing firm in who she is.

As Nadia watches her friends chatting and laughing, she reflects with quiet pride, *"This journey was never about changing for anyone else. It was about discovering that I'm happiest when I'm true to myself. And maybe, just maybe, that's helped others see themselves differently, too."*

Nadia returns to her lunch with a newfound sense of connection—not just to her friends but to her own sense of self. She realizes that the journey brought her something invaluable: respect for herself, an inner confidence, and the understanding that her worth is never defined by fitting into anyone else's standards but her own.

Learning Lessons from True Style

Nadia's story shows you that true style isn't about following trends or fitting into someone else's mold—it's about expressing who you are and feeling proud of it. It's easy to get caught up in worrying about what others think, but just like Nadia, you can discover the power of embracing your own creativity and uniqueness.

When you feel unsure about standing out, remember that taking small steps, like wearing something meaningful or sharing your passions, can help you build confidence. Even if others don't always understand your choices, staying true to yourself is what matters most.

Nadia's journey also reminds you that resilience is key when facing judgment or self-doubt. Having people in your corner, like Ava and Ms. Monroe, can make a big difference, but the strongest validation comes from within. When you focus on what makes you happy and comfortable, you'll realize you don't need anyone else's approval to feel good about yourself.

Finally, sharing your story, like Nadia does with her art project, can inspire others to see the beauty in being themselves. By staying true to who you are, you're not just finding your own confidence—you're showing the world that individuality is something to celebrate.

Story 11 - The Elixir

Devon's life runs like clockwork, every moment dedicated to preserving her flawless reputation. Each morning, her alarm chimes softly, marking the start of another meticulously planned day. Her room mirrors her discipline: a pristine desk, neatly labeled binders, and a corkboard of color-coded sticky notes. To her teachers, she's the gold standard—punctual, polished, always prepared. To her classmates, she's the one to beat, though few even try.

At school, she's known for her perfect grades and polished demeanor, a "model student" in every sense. She thrives on the praise, yet beneath her composed exterior lies a simmering tension—a constant fear that one misstep could shatter the image she's worked so hard to build.

Devon sits at her desk, her pencil flying across the page as she works through a series of challenging math problems. Her planner, marked with neatly checked boxes, sits beside her. It's only mid-morning, and she's already completed her tasks for the day. In front of her, a test with a bold red "100%" lies atop the pile. She picks it up, allowing herself a fleeting smile before setting it back down with a sigh.

"Another A+. That's good... but what about the next one? What if I don't get it right next time? Would they still think I'm the best? Would I?"

The thought sends a ripple of unease through her. Despite the outward success, there's a growing void, a gnawing doubt that no amount of perfect scores seems to fill. Devon's achievements, once a source of pride, now feel like the bare minimum she must maintain to keep her self-worth intact.

The following morning at school, Devon walks into English class, her usual seat by the window waiting for her. The chatter of her classmates blends with the faint sound of chairs scraping against the floor. She pulls out her notebook, its pristine pages a reflection of her need for order.

The usual hum of English class takes a sharp turn when Ms. Harper stands at the front of the room, her warm smile signaling something new. She taps a stack of papers on her desk.

"Today, we're starting a project that's a little different," she begins, her voice carrying a gentle authority. *"I want each of you to write a personal reflection about a time you faced failure and what you learned from it."*

A wave of murmurs spreads through the room as students exchange uneasy glances. Devon sits rigid in her seat, her pen poised above her notebook. Failure? The word alone makes her stomach tighten.

Ms. Harper's tone remains encouraging as she continues, *"This isn't about writing a perfect story. It's about honesty and growth. Sometimes our biggest lessons come from our mistakes."*

Devon's pen moves automatically, jotting down the assignment details, but her mind is already spiraling. She feels the weight of the word *failure* like a stone in her chest. Her carefully curated image has no room for missteps, let alone broadcasting them for others to read.

"Honest? About failure? But what failure?" She feels her pulse quicken. "I've spent my entire life avoiding mistakes. How can I write about something I've worked so hard to prevent?"

As if sensing the class's discomfort, Ms. Harper adds, "Remember, this is a safe space. The point is to explore how challenges help us grow."

Devon forces a nod, but her thoughts remain in turmoil. To her, the idea of sharing a personal failure feels impossible, almost dangerous. Yet, the assignment is non-negotiable, a challenge she can't avoid. It's the first crack in the wall she's built around herself, and deep down, she knows it's just the beginning.

That evening, Devon retreats to her room, determined to tackle the essay. Her laptop glows softly on the neat expanse of her desk. She opens a blank document and rests her hands on the keyboard. But as the cursor blinks, her thoughts spiral, tangled in doubt and fear.

The silence in the house feels deafening, amplifying the internal battle raging within her. Devon types a sentence, pauses, and quickly deletes it. She tries again, but every word feels too raw, too exposing.

The usually calming organization of her room offers no solace. Stacks of color-coded binders sit untouched, a testament to her meticulously controlled world. But this—this assignment—is beyond her control. Her mind spirals.

"What if this essay ruins everything?" Her heart beats faster at the thought. "What if people see me differently—like I'm weak?". The idea makes her stomach churn. "Maybe I could write about that quiz where I lost a couple of points. It's not a real failure, but it's safe... safe and untrue."

The cursor continues its silent, relentless blinking as Devon leans back in her chair, overwhelmed. The weight of expectation bears down on her, and for a moment, she considers closing the laptop altogether. Sharing a real failure feels like stepping into a spotlight she's spent her entire life avoiding.

Her fear isn't just about the assignment—it's about what it represents. For the first time, Devon is being asked to reveal a part of herself she's kept hidden, even from her closest friends. But vulnerability feels like a risk she's not ready to take, and the perfectionist inside her screams for her to find another way.

The next day, the usual rhythm of class feels heavier for Devon. As students gather their belongings at the bell, Ms. Harper's gaze lingers on her.

"Devon, could you stay for a moment?" Ms. Harper asks gently, her tone inviting rather than commanding.

Devon hesitates but nods. Once the classroom clears, an unusual quiet settles in. Ms. Harper leans against her desk, her posture relaxed yet attentive, as if signaling this isn't a typical teacher-student conversation.

Devon sits down, her hands tightly clasped in her lap. The vibrant posters lining the classroom walls, which usually feel motivating, now seem to close in around her.

Ms. Harper gives her a reassuring smile. *"You've been looking a bit preoccupied lately. Is everything alright?"*

Devon's voice falters. *"It's just...this project. I don't know how to write about failure when I've spent my whole life trying to avoid it."*

Ms. Harper nods, her expression thoughtful. *"I get it. But you know, growth doesn't come from always getting it right. It comes from allowing yourself to stumble and finding your way back."*

Devon glances down. *"But what if people think less of me? I'm supposed to be the one who never messes up."*

Ms. Harper's voice softens. *"Devon, real strength isn't about never falling—it's about learning to rise after you do. Let me tell you something: I once completely botched a big presentation early in my teaching career. I was mortified. But that failure taught me resilience and empathy, things that make me a better teacher today."*

Devon couldn't help but wonder: "*She makes it sound like failure can actually lead to something good. But could that be true for me?*"

Ms. Harper's vulnerability plants a seed of hope in Devon. For the first time, she considers the possibility that imperfection doesn't diminish her worth—it may even make her stronger. Though uncertainty still clouds her thoughts, a spark of courage begins to take root.

The next evening, Devon sits at her desk, the laptop's glow highlighting her determined expression. Ms. Harper's words echo in her mind. She begins typing about a hidden moment—the time she turned in an assignment late under intense pressure. The memory stings, but with each word, she feels a growing sense of release.

Devon leans back in her chair, her eyes scanning the draft she's just completed. The room is quiet except for the soft hum of her laptop. For a moment, she feels the weight of her own honesty. It's not perfect, but it's real. She saves the document and closes the laptop gently, a mixture of relief and nervousness washing over her.

She closed her laptop slowly, her mind swirling with unexpected clarity. "*This isn't as terrifying as I thought*", she realized. "*Maybe letting people see I'm not perfect doesn't make me weak. Maybe it makes me real.*"

The act of writing her story marks a turning point. Devon has crossed into uncharted territory, confronting her fear of imperfection head-on. Though her journey is just beginning, this small victory fuels a growing sense of courage.

Devon's world begins to tilt as she faces the reality of her perfectionism. While she tries to maintain her composed exterior, cracks start to show. Her meticulously managed schedule feels heavier, her usual confidence wavering. The first true challenge comes in the form of an 89 on her latest math test—a grade that, to most, would be commendable. But to Devon, it's a glaring failure.

Devon walks into her next class, clutching the paper as if it might crumble under her grip. The bold, red "89" stares back at her, mocking her usual standard of excellence. She slips into her seat, her heart pounding.

Across the table, her friend Harper glances over and notices the score.

Harper: *"An 89? That's awesome, Dev! I'd celebrate if I got that."*

Devon forces a weak smile, her voice light but hollow.

Devon: *"Yeah... it's fine."*

Inside, though, her thoughts spiral. *"Fine? No, it's not fine. I should have done better. What if people think I'm slipping? What if I'm not good enough anymore?"*

As class continues, whispers from nearby students drift her way.

Chloe: *"Devon didn't get an A this time? That's a first."*

Rachel: *"Guess even she can mess up."*

The comments sting more than Devon wants to admit. Each word feels like a confirmation of her worst fears. Harper's reassuring words had briefly soothed her, but they now seem drowned out by her own self-doubt and the weight of expectations.

Devon's gaze drops to her test paper as a knot tightens in her chest. *"Everyone's noticing!"* she thinks, the weight of their whispers pressing down on her. *"I've worked so hard to stay on top, and now one slip-up, and it's like they're ready to watch me fall. If I can't be perfect, what's left?"*

Despite Harper's continued support, Devon begins to isolate herself, retreating further into her thoughts. Every interaction becomes a test, and every glance from her classmates feels like a silent judgment. Her internal struggle intensifies, but she's too afraid to let anyone see the full extent of her fear.

The pressure closes in as the date of the debate competition looms. It's not just another event—it's the kind of stage where Devon is expected to excel, to prove once again that she belongs at the top. But beneath her practiced exterior, doubt gnaws away.

Devon's bedroom, once impeccably organized, now bears the marks of her relentless drive. Debate notes and flashcards are scattered across her desk and bed. The soft hum of her desk lamp casts long shadows, accentuating the dark circles under her eyes. She paces the room, clutching her cards, her voice strained as she rehearses her opening arguments.

Her words falter, and she sinks onto her bed. The weight of exhaustion presses down, heavier than her fear of failing. She glances at the mirror across the room, catching sight of herself—eyes dull, shoulders slumped. The reflection feels unfamiliar, like she's watching a stranger carrying the burden of perfection.

Devon's fingers clutch the edge of a flashcard. *"If I don't get this perfect, what's the point?"* The thought rises, unbidden, sharp like the edge of paper beneath her fingertips. *"They'll see I'm not as capable as they think. I've been holding it together with threads, and now it's all unraveling."*

She pulls her knees to her chest, her eyes flitting between the mess of prep materials and the glow of her phone on the nightstand. A dozen missed messages from her friends go unanswered. Devon feels the tug of isolation as her world narrows to this singular goal: perfection.

But a whisper of fatigue breaks through her storm of thoughts. *"I'm so tired. How much longer can I keep this up?"* It's a quiet admission, one she rarely allows herself to hear, but tonight it lingers, begging for her attention.

Her gaze shifts back to her flashcards, but for once, her hands remain still.

The day of the debate competition arrives, and with it, the crushing weight of Devon's perfectionism. The auditorium buzzes with anticipation as she steps up to the podium, her carefully prepared notes clutched in one hand. She draws a deep breath, scanning the rows of expectant faces. This is her moment, the one she's worked tirelessly for—but beneath the surface, doubt simmers.

Devon begins her argument, her voice steady at first. The points flow seamlessly, and for a moment, she feels in control. But then, she stumbles—a key statistic slips from her mind. Her words falter, and the room seems to shrink, the silence pressing in on her.

Her heart pounds in her ears as she grips the edge of the podium, willing herself to push through. *"Come on, Devon, keep going"*. She takes a steadying breath, forcing her voice to steady as she recalibrates her argument. Her eyes briefly scan the judges' table; their expressions remain neutral, unreadable. The murmurs of the audience fade as she focuses on finishing strong.

Devon regains her rhythm, her words flowing with renewed clarity. She weaves in a compelling rebuttal, her closing points hitting with precision. By the time she steps away from the podium, a smattering of applause rises from the audience. On the surface, she's maintained her poised exterior, but inside, the stumble clings to her—a glaring flaw that overshadows the rest of her performance.

As she walks backstage, fragments of the debate replay in her mind, each highlight accompanied by the shadow of her mistake. It's as though that single falter defines the entire presentation. *"Why couldn't I just get it perfect?"*

Backstage, the adrenaline drains away, leaving her emotionally raw. Devon sinks onto a bench, her hands trembling. The voices from the auditorium fade into a dull hum as tears threaten to spill.

Harper appears, her footsteps soft but deliberate. She sits beside Devon, offering her a water bottle and a kind smile.

Harper: *"You were incredible up there. Seriously, Dev. No one even noticed that little pause."*

Devon: "But I did. It wasn't perfect, Harper. They'll think I'm slipping."

Harper: "*Look, mistakes happen to everyone. What counts is how you handled it—and you handled it like a total pro.*"

Devon looks down, her mind racing. Harper's words are comforting, but the nagging voice in her head refuses to quiet. "*Why can't I let it go?*" she thinks. "*It's like every mistake confirms my worst fears*". Yet, as she reflects on Harper's words, another thought surfaces. "*I finished. I didn't give up*".

For the first time, she begins to consider that resilience might matter more than perfection.

Though she doesn't win first place at the debate competition, Devon's heart skips when the judges announce a special recognition: the "Best Resilience" award. A murmur of surprise ripples through the audience, but Devon feels frozen in place. *Resilience?* The word seems foreign, yet it strikes a chord. Slowly, she rises from her seat, her legs feeling unsteady but her heart beginning to swell.

The spotlight follows Devon as she walks to the stage, her cheeks flushing with a mix of pride and disbelief. The head judge hands her the certificate, smiling warmly.

Judge: "*Devon, your ability to stay composed under pressure today was remarkable. It's not about never making mistakes—it's about how you recover and learn from them.*"

The audience offers a round of applause. Devon takes a deep breath, looking out at the sea of faces.

Devon: "*Thank you. That really means a lot.*"

As she steps down from the stage, the weight of self-imposed expectations begins to lift.

The next day at school, Devon walks through the hallways with a quiet confidence. She notices a few glances but no longer feels defined by them. Harper falls into step beside her, holding out a fist for a playful bump.

Harper: *"See? Told you—you're tougher than you think."*

They walk in comfortable silence for a moment.

Devon: *"I guess I've always thought I had to be perfect for people to respect me. But maybe... it's more about showing up, even when things don't go as planned."*

As she glances around at her peers, Devon feels something shift inside her. *"I've been chasing the wrong goal. It's not about being flawless— it's about having the courage to keep going, even when it's tough."*

She straightens her shoulders, knowing she's carrying something far more valuable than a perfect score—self-acceptance and a newfound resilience that no grade or trophy could ever define.

In the days following the debate, Devon notices a subtle yet profound shift within herself. Though she didn't win first place, the resilience award and the kind words from both the judges and her peers have left an impression. For the first time, she feels the weight of her perfectionism starting to loosen. However, just as she begins to embrace this change, a new challenge arises.

In English class, Ms. Carter stands at the front, her voice calm yet firm as she announces the next project.

Ms. Carter: *"Your next assignment is a reflective essay titled A Lesson from My Biggest Mistake. This is an opportunity to explore a moment when things didn't go as planned and what you learned from it."*

The class murmurs, exchanging glances. Devon freezes in her seat, her mind racing.

Later that evening, she sits at her desk, staring at a blank document on her laptop. Her fingers hover over the keyboard, hesitant to type. A safer topic—a minor mistake no one would judge her for—tempts her. But Mr. Blake's words from the debate echo in her mind: *"Growth comes from embracing what challenges us."*

Devon leans back, her gaze drifting toward the ceiling. *"If I'm honest, this could change how people see me. But maybe... that's not such a bad thing. Maybe it's time they know I'm not perfect—and that's okay."*

With a steadying breath, she begins to type. The words flow as she recounts her experience at the debate, the moment she faltered, and the strength it took to keep going. She writes about how that stumble taught her that resilience matters more than flawless execution,, that real courage is found in the recovery.

As she types, Devon feels an unexpected sense of release. Each sentence feels like shedding an old layer of herself, one built on rigid expectations and fear of judgment. This essay isn't just an assignment; it's a declaration of her newfound understanding: her worth isn't tied to perfection, but to her authenticity and growth.

The day of the essay presentations arrives, and Devon's hands tremble slightly as she clutches her paper. The familiar weight of anxiety presses down, but she steadies herself with a deep breath. She watches her classmates take their turns, her pulse quickening as her name is finally called. With quiet resolve, she rises and walks to the front of the room.

The classroom hums with anticipation as Devon stands behind the podium. Her voice starts soft but grows steadier as she begins reading. She shares the suffocating pressure of being labeled the "perfect student," the burnout that followed, and the fear of losing herself in the process.

Her voice wavers momentarily when she reaches the part about the debate—the stumble, the panic, the weight of self-doubt. But she pushes through, her words carrying a newfound conviction.

Devon: *"...and that's when I realized, it wasn't about never making mistakes. It was about how I chose to move forward despite them.'*

She pauses, scanning the room. The silence is heavy, but not with judgment. It's understanding.

Anna, sitting near the front, breaks the quiet with a gentle smile.

Anna: *"Devon, I had no idea you felt that way. It's really brave of you to share."*

From across the room, Jacob nods in agreement.

Jacob: *"Honestly, same here. I've been trying to keep up this perfect image, but it's exhausting. Hearing you talk about it... it helps."*

Devon's shoulders relax as warmth spreads through her. She glances toward Harper, who gives her an enthusiastic thumbs-up. Even Emily, usually composed and distant, offers a small, thoughtful nod.

As Devon returns to her seat, her thoughts swirl. *"Maybe I've been looking at this all wrong. I don't have to carry this alone—others understand more than I ever realized."*

For the first time, Devon feels lighter, as though the armor she's worn for so long has finally started to crack, letting in light. Sharing her truth hasn't diminished her in anyone's eyes; it's strengthened her connection to those around her.

This marks a turning point—not just in how Devon views herself, but in how she navigates the world, embracing vulnerability as a source of true strength.

Later that day, during lunch, Devon sits with Harper and Jacob, the hum of the cafeteria surrounding them. The conversation flows easily, a stark contrast to the tension she once felt trying to uphold her "perfect" image. Today, they're talking about their own experiences with academic pressure, trading strategies for managing stress and finding balance.

Harper: *"Honestly, I've started setting a timer when I study. When it goes off, I force myself to take a break. It helps keep me sane."*

Jacob: *"Same here. I stopped studying until midnight. Turns out, sleep actually works."*

Devon chuckles, realizing she's not alone in these struggles.

Devon: *"I've been trying to set limits too. It's a work in progress, but I'm getting there."*

As their laughter fades, Mr. Blake walks past their table, pausing when he spots Devon. His expression is warm and proud.

Mr. Blake: *"Devon, I heard about your presentation this morning. That's the kind of courage that sparks real change."*

Devon feels a swell of pride.

Devon: *"Thanks, Mr. Blake. I've learned it's not about being perfect— it's about being real."*

Mr. Blake nods, satisfied: *"Exactly. Keep leading by example."*

As Mr. Blake walks away, Devon looks around at her friends. She feels lighter, more at ease than she has in months. A thought takes shape, clear and affirming. *"This journey wasn't about proving my worth through perfect scores. It was about learning to value myself— imperfections and all—and showing others they can too."*

Devon now carries the "elixir" of self-compassion and balance. It's a gift she's determined to nurture, not just for herself, but for those around her. She knows her story doesn't end here; it's a beginning, a foundation for a life built on authenticity and resilience.

With her friends by her side and her mentor's words echoing in her heart, Devon smiles. She's no longer defined by unattainable standards. She's thriving as her most honest, imperfect self.

Learning Lessons from "The Elixir"

You don't need to be perfect to be worthy, strong, or admired. Devon's story reminds you that true strength isn't about avoiding mistakes but about how you rise after making them. Everyone stumbles, but it's in those moments of vulnerability that you discover your real courage. It's okay to admit when things don't go as planned—it's part of being human.

Letting go of perfectionism doesn't mean letting go of ambition; it means giving yourself permission to grow and learn without the fear of judgment. When Devon embraced her missteps, she found not only self-acceptance but also deeper connections with those around her. The same can be true for you—sharing your struggles can inspire others and remind you that you're not alone.

This story also teaches you the value of resilience. Life isn't about getting everything right; it's about moving forward even when things feel uncertain. If you stop tying your self-worth to flawless outcomes, you'll find more joy, balance, and authenticity in everything you do.

Remember, your worth isn't defined by perfection. It's in your willingness to try, to learn, and to keep going no matter what. And that's more than enough.

To Bring with You

As you close this book, take a moment to reflect on the journeys you've just experienced. Each character, with their unique struggles and triumphs, has walked a path of growth—one that might feel familiar to your own. Whether they faced perfectionism, self-doubt, or the pressure to fit in, their stories share a common truth: strength is found not in chasing an ideal but in embracing who you are, imperfections and all.

The Lessons We've Learned

Through their adventures, these characters have shown us that life's challenges aren't roadblocks—they're stepping stones. Here are some truths you can carry with you:

- **Mistakes Are Part of the Journey:** Devon, Aria, and the others have learned that setbacks don't define their worth. Whether it's a stumble in a debate or a struggle to fit in, every challenge is an opportunity to grow. When you face your own missteps, remember: they are simply lessons in disguise.
- **Self-Worth Comes from Within:** In a world that often measures success by achievements or appearance, it's easy to lose sight of what truly matters. But as these stories remind us, your value isn't tied to external validation. It comes from embracing your unique strengths and showing up as your authentic self.
- **Connection is a Source of Strength:** Throughout their journeys, the characters found support in unexpected places—a mentor's wisdom, a friend's encouragement, or even their own reflection. You don't have to face life's challenges alone. Trust in the people who see your potential, and don't be afraid to lean on them when you need it.

Your Own Hero's Journey

Every day, you're writing your own story. Like the characters in this book, you'll face trials that test your courage and resilience. Some days will be harder than others, but every step forward—no matter how small—counts.

- **Embrace Your Journey:** There's no single path to self-confidence or success. Your journey will be as unique as you are. Celebrate your progress, and give yourself grace on the days when it feels like you're standing still.
- **Define Success on Your Terms:** The world will always have expectations, but you have the power to decide what success means for you. Is it about grades? Friendships? Exploring your creativity? Whatever it is, let it be something that brings you joy and fulfillment.
- **Remember: You're Enough:** Not because of what you achieve, how you look, or how others perceive you. You're enough simply because you are.

A Final Thought

As you step back into your own life, know that every story—yours included—is a work in progress. There will be highs and lows, triumphs and setbacks. But with each experience, you're growing stronger, wiser, and more in tune with your true self.

Carry these stories with you as a reminder of your resilience, your worth, and your potential. When doubt creeps in, let the voices of these characters remind you: you're capable of far more than you think.

Now, it's your turn to be the hero of your own journey. Embrace the adventure, trust in your strength, and never forget—you are always enough.

The Next Chapter Awaits

The book may end here, but your story continues. Take what you've learned, apply it in your own life, and know that you have everything you need to thrive. Go forward with courage, confidence, and the knowledge that your journey is yours to shape.

To bring with you wherever you go in life: hope, courage, and the unwavering belief in your own potential.

About the Authors

At Aria Capri Publishing, we are dedicated to fostering fun and growth through learning for children and teens. Our mission is to empower young minds to explore their unique journeys, embrace their potential, and trust in their ability to grow. With an open mind and a spirit of curiosity, every child and teen can take steps toward a brighter future.

We know young people are natural learners—eager and ready to absorb knowledge in their own way. Recognizing that there's no one-size-fits-all approach to personal growth, we create interactive books rooted in science-backed research. Our goal is to nurture developing minds while inspiring confidence, resilience, and a lifelong love of learning.

As parents ourselves, we understand your desire to see your children and teens thrive. That's why our books are designed to support readers of all ages in building a growth mindset and realizing their unique potential.

We're Mauricio and Devon, a husband-and-wife team with a shared passion for lifelong learning and personal growth. After the birth of our daughter, Aria Capri, we were inspired to create something meaningful—not just for her but for families everywhere. Aria is our muse, our motivation, and the namesake of this publishing group. Together, we're committed to helping children and teens grow into their brightest, most confident selves.

Thank You for Reading!

We hope this book has inspired confidence and growth for the teen girl in your life. If you found value in these stories, we'd love to hear your thoughts! Your review can help others discover this book and make a difference in the lives of more young readers.

To leave a review, simply scan the QR code below or visit the platform where you purchased this book. Your support as a reader means everything and helps us continue creating empowering content.

Thank you for being part of this journey!

Warm regards,

Devon & Mauricio